I0812554

MONSTER HUNTING

Hunting the Headless Horseman

MARK LATHAM

ROSEN PUBLISHING
New York

This edition published in 2017 by

The Rosen Publishing Group, Inc.
29 East 21st Street
New York, NY 10010

Additional end matter copyright © 2017 by The Rosen Publishing Group, Inc.

All rights reserved. No part of this book may be reproduced in any form without permission in writing from the publisher, except by a reviewer.

Library of Congress Cataloging-in-Publication Data

Names: Latham, Mark (Wargamer), author. | Irving, Washington, 1783-1859. Legend of Sleepy Hollow.
Title: Hunting the Headless Horseman / Mark Latham.
Description: New York : Rosen Publishing, 2017. | Series: Monster hunting
Identifiers: LCCN 2016035770 | ISBN 9781499465365 (library bound)
Subjects: LCSH: Ghosts.
Classification: LCC BF1471 .L38 2016 | DDC 133.1/4—dc23
LC record available at https://lccn.loc.gov/2016035770

Manufactured in the United States of America

© Osprey Publishing, 2015
All rights reserved

This edition published by Rosen Publishing by arrangement with Osprey Publishing, an imprint of Bloomsbury Publishing Plc.

Contents

Introduction

> *"Faith, sir," replied the story-teller, "as to that matter, I don't believe one-half of it myself."*
>
> - D.K.

The Legend of Sleepy Hollow has long held a fascination for scholars of the supernatural, and, more commonly, those who study the rise of the "urban legend." For this short tale by acclaimed American author Washington Irving, based on snatches of folklore and ghost stories from the Dutch settlement of Tarrytown, New York, is widely believed to be a fiction, dreamt up from Irving's vivid imagination. That it has come to capture the public imagination, becoming known as a real slice of American folk mythology rather than a mere story, is testament to the power of the narrative. Parallels may well be drawn between Sleepy Hollow and the British tale of *Sweeney Todd, the Demon Barber of Fleet Street* – another fictional character widely believed to have existed in old London town.

But what if *The Legend of Sleepy Hollow*, and its grim story of the unfortunate schoolteacher Ichabod Crane, was not a fiction at all? What if, in the tradition of his peers across the world, Washington Irving had stumbled upon a supernatural truth, an esoteric mystery so dark as to defy the rationale of everyday folk? Wrapped in the disguise of a storybook, *The Legend of Sleepy Hollow* merely hints at the true nature of the Headless Horseman. For these ghastly spirits are not just found in the state of New York, nor even on American soil. Headless spirits are a unique, sentient form of wraith, and tales of their terrifying exploits have been recorded since the Early Middle Ages.

The book you hold in your hands uncovers certain uncomfortable truths. Truths that reveal the Headless Horseman, and others like him, to be at large in the dark places of the world. Should one encounter a headless spirit of this type, then it is said that tragedy will surely follow, for the one common thread of all the tales of headless spirits is that they are harbingers of evil and dismay. For most common folk, it is better to go through life not knowing of the existence of these fell entities. If you are such a soul, better to close this book now than to have the safe haven of ignorance torn from you. But if you are of a more intrepid mind, and would rather have the truth at any cost, then read on, if you dare …

Chapter 1 - Sleepy Hollow

From the listless repose of the place, and the peculiar character of its inhabitants, who are descendants from the original Dutch settlers, this sequestered glen has long been known by the name of Sleepy Hollow ... A drowsy, dreamy influence seems to hang over the land, and to pervade the very atmosphere.

Our story begins not at the very origins of the headless spirits, but at the site of their most famous haunt: Sleepy Hollow itself, which lies in the valley of the Pocantico River, a small stream that flows into the Hudson. It was in this remote settlement that Washington Irving, following in the footsteps of the real Ichabod Crane, encountered the malevolent horseman. Assuming the *nom de plume* of storyteller "Diedrich Knickerbocker," Irving penned the tale of Crane's exploits, hoping it would serve as a grim warning to future generations. Had he known that one day his writings would be laughed off as a harmless ghost story, he might have reconsidered his approach. For now, however, let us examine the tale, as told by Irving so long ago, and its ghastly message.

The Legend

The old country wives, however, who are the best judges of these matters, maintain to this day that Ichabod was spirited away by supernatural means; and it is a favorite story often told about the neighborhood round the winter evening fire. The bridge became more than ever an object of superstitious awe; and that may be the reason why the road has been altered of late years, so as to approach the church by the border of the millpond. The schoolhouse being deserted soon fell to decay, and was reported to be haunted by the ghost of the unfortunate pedagogue and the plowboy, loitering homeward of a still summer evening, has often fancied his voice at a distance, chanting a melancholy psalm tune among the tranquil solitudes of Sleepy Hollow.

Irving's famous "legend" relates the tale of Ichabod Crane, a schoolteacher from Connecticut, and his adventures in Sleepy Hollow. This secluded glen is situated in the countryside around the Dutch settlement of Tarrytown, and was renowned for its ghosts and superstitions long before the arrival of Crane. The most infamous specter of the region was, of course, the Headless

Horseman – thought to be the restless spirit of a Hessian artilleryman, killed during "some nameless battle" of the American Revolutionary War, and who rode abroad "to the scene of the battle in nightly quest for his head."

When Ichabod Crane arrived in Sleepy Hollow, he fell in love with Katrina Van Tassel (in reality Catriena Van Tassel), the sole daughter of wealthy farmer Baltus Van Tassel, and set about attempting to win her hand. However, his rival for the affections of Katrina was local hero and rowdy Abraham Van Brunt, known locally as "Brom Bones." Crane was a jittery, superstitious man, and before long Brom took advantage of his rival's nervous nature by playing a series of practical jokes upon him, making Crane – a Yankee and an outsider – look foolish at every opportunity.

Baltus Van Tassel's fortune was the greatest in the area, and Katrina was thus the most eligible young woman in Sleepy Hollow. Though by modern standards it paints his protagonist in a poor light, Irving was clear that Ichabod

By the time Irving came to write his tale, his opinion of strict schoolmaster Ichabod Crane was somewhat low. Irving wrote: *"To see him striding along the profile of a hill on a windy day, with his clothes bagging and fluttering about him, one might have mistaken him for the genius of famine descending upon the earth, or some scarecrow eloped from a cornfield."*

Crane coveted Katrina's dowry as much as her love. With this in mind, Ichabod attended a harvest party at the Van Tassel home, where he danced, feasted, and listened to ghost stories told by the locals. When the party-goers finally went home, Ichabod stayed behind and proposed to Katrina, but was refused. Crestfallen, Ichabod returned home, riding through the woods between the farmstead and Sleepy Hollow late at night.

Ichabod, his imagination fired up by the stories told that night, was in a nervous state. Passing beneath a lightning-stricken tulip tree – itself a haunted spot – Ichabod reached at last an intersection in the road, in the midst of a swamp. There, he encountered a horseman, cloaked and silent, and upon closer inspection realized that the stranger's head was not on his shoulders, but instead lashed to his saddle. Ichabod spurred on his horse and fled, aiming for the bridge next to the Old Dutch Burial Ground, where it was said the Hessian would vanish upon crossing. Making it at last to the bridge, Ichabod urged his plough-horse across, and turned in horror to see the Headless Horseman crossing also. There was no flash of fire and brimstone as the legend suggested – instead, the Hessian reared his horse and flung his flaming head at Ichabod's face, unseating the schoolmaster at once.

The next morning, Ichabod Crane was nowhere to be found. Indeed, the only traces of him at all were his wandering horse, trampled hat, and remnants of a shattered pumpkin. Brom Bones was thus free to marry Katrina, and the story as written clearly implicates him in the disappearance of Ichabod Crane. Yet, even if Brom had dressed up as the Hessian and used a jack o'lantern as a "severed head," was he really the sort of man to dispose of a weaker opponent so cruelly?

If we take Washington Irving's tale as more than a mere fiction, it begs the questions – what happened to Ichabod? And who bore witness to tell the tale to Irving?

Irving and Crane: Ghost Hunters

The reality of the story is perhaps even stranger than fiction. From secret journals long suppressed, we know now that Washington Irving traveled to Sleepy Hollow in the early part of 1799 as a teenager, having come across the tale of the Headless Horseman in the library at Tarrytown. Three years later, he began to carve out a reputation for himself as a keen folklorist and essayist. In the years to come, Washington Irving would become something more, too: a psychical investigator, one of the earliest known proponents of the application of scientific method in discovering and monitoring supernatural phenomena.

This strange – and secret – pursuance of a career little known was not an accidental turn. In Sleepy Hollow, the young Irving had heard the strange tale of the disappearance of a schoolmaster named Crane. Irving had the chance to meet Katrina Van Tassel – now Mrs Van Brunt – for himself, and hear the story from her own lips. Resourceful even at such a young age, Washington persuaded the elders of the glen to let him see Ichabod Crane's possessions –

never claimed of course. Amongst them were several books on diverse topics, from folklore and occult philosophy to "psychical phenomena," and it was these books that would fire Washington Irving's imagination for some time to come. Even more fantastic, however, was a fat, leather-wrapped journal written in Crane's own hand, and retained in the possession of Katrina Van Brunt. Irving used all of his guile and part of his modest allowance to procure the book, which was written largely in shorthand and decorated with sigils and signs of occult provenance. The elders, naturally, believed that Crane had dabbled in satanic rituals, and had perhaps brought the Horseman down upon himself in so doing. But Irving did not believe that was the full story. When later he returned to New York, it was with a new field of study in mind.

Upon reaching his 18th birthday, Irving was invited to join a private and highly secretive gentlemen's club in New York City, the Lycean. This chapter of Irving's life has been hitherto undocumented, but membership of this society

Washington Irving, *c.*1842, after a long and successful career battling the supernatural.

opened many doors for the young folklorist, and within the vast library and archive room of the club he began to decipher Crane's journal, and piece together the truth about Sleepy Hollow. It seemed that Crane himself had been a member of the Lycean, and had set off to Sleepy Hollow incognito, on the business of "psychical research." Once there, he had fallen for a local girl, which compromised his investigation and unwittingly made him a target for the ill-will of the locals. The magical wards and charms detailed in Crane's journal were evidence, Irving believed, that Crane thought the Headless Horseman to be controlled by one or more of the locals. By the end, Crane was desperate, believing himself to be a target of the Horseman. When he attended the Van Tassel gathering, it had not been solely to win Katrina's hand, but to entice her to flee with him before the Horseman rode abroad. This had formed the basis of the last journal entry, written just hours before Crane's fateful ride into the woods near Sleepy Hollow.

When Irving presented these findings to senior figures at the Lycean, he was hurriedly inducted into a mysterious agency, operating from within the club. There, Irving was shown secrets handed to the club from agents in Europe and the Middle East, charting supernatural phenomena across the globe. He devoured the esoteric teachings of Franz Anton Mesmer, and read suppressed fragments of the Books of Grimm – essays by two brothers living in Germany that contained disturbing truths rather than fanciful fiction. In particular, a series of letters written to the Lycean by Jacob Grimm made reference to the headless Grey Huntsman of Germany, which was renowned as a harbinger of doom. Irving discovered a world beyond the realm of the physical – a world in which ghosts and goblins existed, and long-dead Hessian horsemen could ride through darkened forests of a night, compelled by some unknown force.

There was little doubt in Irving's mind that, now armed with occult secrets and glimpses of a terrible truth, only one course of action was available to him. He must return to Sleepy Hollow.

The Hessian

How often did he shrink with curdling awe at the sound of his own steps on the frosty crust beneath his feet; and dread to look over his shoulder, lest he should behold some uncouth being tramping close behind him! And how often was he thrown into complete dismay by some rushing blast, howling among the trees, in the idea that it was the Galloping Hessian on one of his nightly scourings!

Irving's first recourse was to research the Horseman himself, for the young "psychical detective" believed the key to unraveling the mystery of Sleepy Hollow lay in understanding who the phantom rider was in life.

The libraries in New York and Tarrytown – even that of the Lycean – were of little use, telling Irving only what he already knew. The Hessian was an artilleryman in a mercenary regiment, sent to the Americas in the employ of the British. At White Plains, the nameless soldier had been killed by a stray cannon-shot, his head struck from his shoulders in an instant. Yet many died that day at White Plains, so why should this lowly artilleryman have been singled out for ghostly resurrection?

Irving became obsessed with his studies, making several trips to Tarrytown and Sleepy Hollow over the months that followed. In Sleepy Hollow he questioned the locals as subtly as he could, gathering clues as to the identity of the Hessian. Irving sent several missives to the Apollonian Club of London – the twin institution of New York's Lycean – and received by return post a collection of army reports of the Hessian forces that served at White Plains. Several likely candidates for the true identity of the Horseman presented themselves, and Irving used this information to assist in his discreet inquiries.

He learned that the Hessian had been an officer in the light artillery, hence

Reviled by friend and foe alike for their uncompromising tactics and insular command structure, the Hessians were hardy mercenaries.

the horse. The officer was carried away by his compatriots, and buried in the Old Dutch cemetery at Sleepy Hollow, though the head – sundered by the cannonball – was not recovered. Irving also discovered that the head was never found, but learned of another local legend that told of battlefield scavengers picking White Plains clean when the fighting was done, and placing the heads of the fallen enemy on stakes along the road from Singsing to Tarrytown, as a warning to British forces in the future. Though most of these heads were eventually gathered and buried with the dead in a mass grave near the Old Dutch Church, some were never recovered. Though he could not be certain which version of events presented the truth, Irving surmised that, in death, the Hessian was never reunited with his head, presenting a cause for his nightly wanderings.

Irving spoke to several elderly residents of Sleepy Hollow who had been alive at the time of the infamous battle, chief amongst them an old widow who lived alone on the edge of the glen. Shunned by the other villagers amidst rumors of witchcraft, the widow nevertheless provided much of interest to the inquisitive young writer. Correlating her tales with the notes in Crane's journal, Washington Irving began to piece together a picture of the Hessian's life and last days that shone new and disturbing light upon the accepted facts.

The picture painted of the Hessian by the octogenarian widow was one of a savage bully, who had traveled with his German compatriots not merely for the coin of his paymasters, but for the love of slaughter. The Hessian had not been trained as an artilleryman originally, but had instead been a sapper – a front-line assault trooper deployed to erect defensive lines and destroy enemy fortifications. Armed with axe and sword, these "engineers" were often large, aggressive men who excelled at close-quarter fighting, and Irving's Hessian, it seemed, was no exception. His blood-lust became so noted during the American campaign that the Hessian was almost sent home in disgrace after butchering whole families and collecting grizzly trophies. Unlike his fellows, he was said to maintain a ferocious appearance, his hair tousled, his teeth filed to points the better to bite his foes savagely, and his uniform replaced almost entirely with non-regulation black clothing found on campaign.

Irving spent many hours with the old widow, listening to her tales of the Hessian. He learned how, at the Battle of Long Island, the soldier had been decorated for valor, winning a field promotion. Even then his vicious streak should have been noted – the decoration was won because the Hessian, while storming the American barricades, had single-handedly slain a dozen regulars in a display of martial prowess so fearsome that half a company had fled the sight of it. That the Hessian had dismembered his enemies after death like slaughtered cattle, until his uniform was blood-scarlet, was ignored in the glow of victory.

After that first battle, the Hessian was allegedly engaged in a fight with one of his English allies. The English mistrusted the German troops, and this enmity often spilled over into violence in camp. On this particular occasion, three English subalterns, drunk after receiving the spoils of war, waylaid the

(Opposite)
Sleepy Hollow Horseman
"On mounting a rising ground, which brought the figure of his fellow-traveller in relief against the sky, gigantic in height, and muffled in a cloak, Ichabod was horror-struck on perceiving that he was headless!--but his horror was still more increased on observing that the head, which should have rested on his shoulders, was carried before him on the pommel of his saddle!"
– The Legend of Sleepy Hollow

Hessian. The German, supposedly not understanding his tormentors, became enraged and killed one of the men, half hacking off the subaltern's head with a "hanger," or stubby cutlass. Having just the previous day received an honor for bravery, the Hessian was acquitted of any wrongdoing, although relations between the English and Hessian troops continued to be strained throughout the campaign.

The Hessian's activities were recorded again in the bitter skirmish at Harlem Heights (September 16, 1776). During the early stages of the battle, Lieutenant Colonel Knowlton and his famous Rangers almost outflanked the British forces, but for a last-minute mistake which signaled their presence to the Hessian vanguard. The British and German alliance quickly responded to the maneuver and attacked Knowlton's Rangers. The Hessian was foremost amongst the counterattacking force, and legend has it that he tore into Knowlton's riflemen with unbridled aggression. Knowlton himself was killed that day, and rumors persist that his throat was torn out, though whether the

THE BATTLE OF WHITE PLAINS

This battle of the American Revolutionary War took place on October 28, 1776. Following the retreat of George Washington's army northward from New York City, British general William Howe landed troops in Westchester County, intending to cut off Washington's escape route. Wise to this move, Washington retreated farther, establishing a position in the village of White Plains.

The Battle of White Plains is often viewed as a pause in a long retreat. Positioning his army on the hills around White Plains, Washington decided to make a stand against General Howe, whose regiments were advancing from New Rochelle and Scarsdale. The southern anchor of Washington's defensive line was at Chatterton Hill, and the line failed to hold. Enemy forces in British red and Hessian blue charged up the hill from the Bronx River, and though the first few waves were repulsed, the superior enemy force finally drove the Continental troops from the hilltop. With the loss of the hill, Washington was forced to retreat, abandoning his defensive lines.

At the time, the defeat seemed to be another dismal episode in the collapse of Washington's army, but in retrospect, the most important aspect of the Battle of White Plains was seen to be not the American defeat, but Washington's ability to prevent envelopment by General Howe's forces, withdraw his troops in good order, and preserve the army for a more propitious day – notably at the battles of Princeton and Trenton.

Though both armies numbered more than 13,000 men, the reality was that only about 4,000 soldiers participated in the battle itself. By the time the dust had cleared, the British counted an official casualty list of 313 against less than 300 for the Americans.

injuries were sustained before or after death – and whether they were inflicted by man or beast – have never been confirmed.

The American forces continued the fight until they ran out of ammunition, at which point they were forced to leave the field. Upon their retreat, the Hessian and a small group of mercenaries defied orders and pursued the American forces, hacking apart any they caught. Again, the Hessian's superiors turned a blind eye, choosing to focus on the sapper's formidable skill in battle rather than his violent excesses. Yet very soon they would have no choice but to address their soldier's behavior.

Later that night, the English soldiery descended upon local farmsteads and settlements, razing homes to the ground, defiling and pillaging where they could. The Hessians had rarely partaken in such activity, looking upon it with disdain, especially as many of the people on the East Coast were of German origin too. However, the Hessian snuck out of camp that night and joined the drunken English. His mission was not to drink hard liquor and make free with local girls. No, his mission was one of wanton murder and bloodshed, and this time he was discovered.

The Hessian was found in a farmhouse some three miles from the British camp, surrounded by death. The provosts apprehended him, and one was wounded in the attempt, but there was no denying his crimes. The Hessian had killed an entire family – women, children, youths, and patriarch – butchering them and gnawing at their flesh. The provosts described the man as a "rabid animal," and recommended that he be hanged. The Hessian command staff, however, embarrassed that one of their celebrated "heroes" could have stooped so low, showed leniency. Placing the Hessian in charge of a battery of horse artillery where he would be away from the thick of the fighting, they thought they could harness his skill at arms while curbing his penchant for blood. Little did they know that they had merely consigned their man to an untimely death after all.

That death, at the Battle of White Plains, was not the end of the Hessian's story. Irving presented his theories about the lost heads of the defeated British and Hessian soldiers to the old widow, who cackled with laughter at the suggestion. The head of the Hessian, she maintained, had not been "lost," but stolen, for some dark purpose!

This revelation plunged Washington Irving into a new line of inquiry. The idea that the Headless Horseman was not some aimless wraith attacking at random, but was instead being controlled – directed against living targets – was discomfiting indeed. Irving at once returned to the history and folklore of Sleepy Hollow, unearthing evidence of witchcraft and demonology stretching back to the earliest days of the colony and even farther still, to the time of the Oneida Indian Nation. Before the Dutch had arrived with their superstitions, the land was already replete with native burial grounds and steeped in "medicine" from the long-held enmity between the Oneida and the Mohawk tribes. Irving learned of a long, dark history, which he felt sure made Sleepy

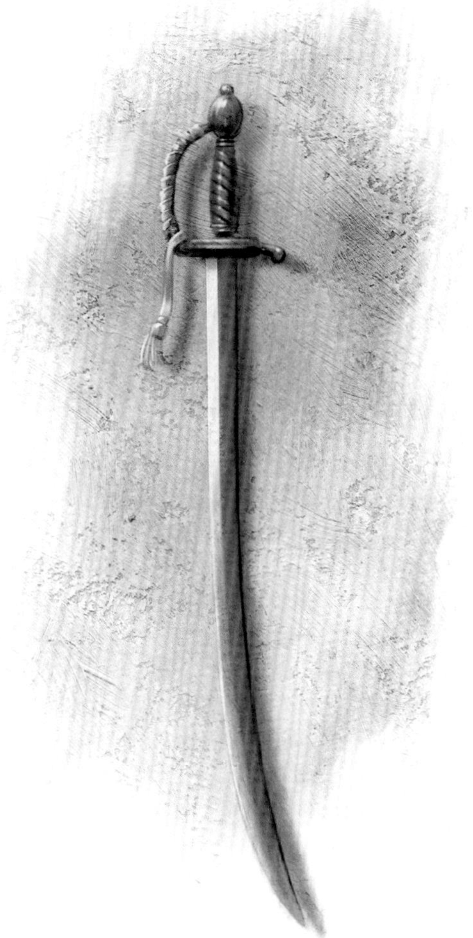

The Headless Horseman was reported to use any weapon that came to hand, though he always favored the long artillery officer's sword that he carried in life.

Hollow a place of deep magical resonance – a fact that would work in the favor of anyone determined to employ black magic to further their own ends.

Over the course of his investigations, Irving had made a cordial acquaintanceship with the Van Tassel family, and one or two of the lesser families in Sleepy Hollow. Though many of the townsfolk still mistrusted him as a stranger and potential "spy" in their midst – not lessened when they discovered his English heritage – Irving now exploited the few friendships he had made to investigate the recorded history of the area. Campfire tales and yarns spun by isolated old widows were one thing, but if Irving was to pit himself against a great evil, he knew he must be armed with facts. Irving resolved first to look for a pattern in the prior hauntings of the Horseman, and thence to compare that pattern to what he knew of the intertwined fortunes of the great households of Sleepy Hollow. Once he had established motive and opportunity, he could perhaps identify the culprit and lay the restless spirit once and for all.

Victims of the Horseman

> *Indeed, certain of the most authentic historians of those parts, who have been careful in collecting and collating the floating facts concerning this specter, allege that the body of the trooper having been buried in the church-yard, the ghost rides forth to the scene of battle in nightly quest of his head; and that the rushing speed with which he sometimes passes along the Hollow, like a midnight blast, is owing to his being belated, and in a hurry to get back to the church-yard before daybreak.*

Between 1779 and 1799, there had been 13 recorded sightings of the Headless Horseman of Sleepy Hollow. One of those sightings was found in a magistrate's court transcript of 1781, and was disregarded at the time due to the alleged drunkenness of the witness. Of the remaining 12, Irving noted that the majority – eight, in fact – were not specifically tied to murder or disappearance, nor to any other suggestion of foul play. The Horseman, in each instance, had merely been seen abroad, riding across the glen on his "demonic black steed." Sometimes, he had in hand a jack o'lantern, as he supposedly had when pursuing the unfortunate Ichabod Crane. However, closer inspection of records from the Old Dutch Church showed that, just a day or two after each sighting of the Horseman, some calamity befell the town.

In one instance, a young boy drowned in the creek; in another, a family was killed in a terrible fire; the worst of all came when the yellow fever came to Sleepy Hollow in 1793, killing 21 people. The first symptoms were noted just days after the Hessian's ghost was seen galloping by Raven Rock.

The remaining encounters with the Horseman – and the most recent – were more sinister still. Beginning with the wealthiest local landowner, Peter Van Garrett, the Horseman had seemingly ceased foreshadowing tragedy and become instead an angel of death – a phantasmal killer. Van Garrett was found out on the Tarrytown trail, his carriage shattered, and the coachman dead at the reins. Van Garrett's head had been struck from his shoulders. Although some tried to claim it was a dreadful accident, there were few in Sleepy Hollow who doubted that the Horseman had struck. Sure enough, less than one week later, a village watchman reported that he had seen the Hessian riding furiously in the direction of the Van Garrett manor, "as though the very hounds o' hell were with him." That night, during a violent storm, Peter Van Garrett's son and heir was killed. The huge double doors of the family home were battered down, with great hoof-marks impressed within

THE GHOSTS OF SLEEPY HOLLOW

Several of the Sleepy Hollow people were present at Van Tassel's, and, as usual, were doling out their wild and wonderful legends. Many dismal tales were told about funeral trains, and mourning cries and wailings heard and seen about the great tree where the unfortunate Major André was taken, and which stood in the neighborhood. Some mention was made also of the woman in white, that haunted the dark glen at Raven Rock, and was often heard to shriek on winter nights before a storm, having perished there in the snow.

As alluded to in the fictionalized account of Crane's exploits, there is more spectral activity in the sinister glen of Sleepy Hollow than just the Hessian. Though the Horseman is the most notorious – and deadly – apparition to have haunted the environs of Sleepy Hollow, Washington Irving realized that the frequent appearance of other specters must surely indicate the region's singular supernatural properties.

Raven Rock in particular is a remote, shadow-haunted place, so remote that it is known only to a few locals. The rock is in a dark and foreboding glen on the east side of Buttermilk Hill, southeast of Ferguson Lake. Legend tells us that three ghosts, not just Irving's lady in white, roam the area. The lady in white was a girl, who got lost in a snowstorm and sought shelter from the fierce wind by the rock, but the snow drifted in and she perished during the night. It is believed that the spirit of the lady meets the wanderer with cries that resemble the howling of the wind, and gestures that remind one of drifting snow, warning all to stay away from the fatal spot.

A more ancient legend tells of an Indian maid who was driven to her death by a jealous lover. Her spirit is believed to roam the area, lamenting her fate. The third spirit is that of a colonial girl, who fled from the attentions of an amorous raider during the Revolution, and leapt from the rock to her death.

Perhaps more famously, the area known as Wiley's Swamp – on the border between Sleepy Hollow and Tarrytown – is known for harboring the ghost of Major John André, a British spy captured by three local militiamen. André was part of American general Benedict Arnold's treasonous plan to hand the defenses at West Point – and George Washington himself – over to the British, which would have resulted in a very different outcome of the Revolution! The ill-fated André was later hanged, but his spirit lingers around the spot where he was captured. Wiley's Swamp is a thickly wooded grove, with a stream running through it, crossed by a simple log bridge. It is here that the Horseman was first encountered by Ichabod Crane, and where Irving felt the unmistakable redolence of esoteric power coursing through the very earth.

the lacquered wood. A maid, traumatized by the experience, recalled how the Headless Horseman used a wood-axe from the yard, and cleaved the younger Van Garrett's head from his shoulders like so much firewood.

The third victim was, of course, Ichabod Crane, whose body was never found at all, though some whispered that he had been the victim of his rival for the hand of Katrina Van Tassel, Brom Bones. Irving naturally believed Brom to be controlling the Horseman, or else embroiled somehow in a pernicious scheme, but a doubt crept into his mind when the fourth victim was claimed during Irving's stay in the settlement. This time, the victim was none other than the wife of Baltus Van Tassel – Brom's own mother-in-law – Maria. With a recent death in the family, the Van Tassels could not be easily accused of dabbling in dark magic, and so Irving knew he would have to tread carefully if he was to expose those responsible for unleashing the Horseman.

(Opposite)
Dismounted during his running battle with Washington Irving, the Horseman still proved a sinister and implacable foe.

Chapter 2 - Hunting the Horseman

Washington Irving began his investigation with the recently appointed magistrate, Samuel Philipse. Belonging to an old family (indeed, his grandfather built the Old Dutch Church), Philipse had replaced Peter Van Garrett as local magistrate upon his death. Irving noted with interest that the Philipse family had once been the wealthiest in the area, having owned the manor house until it was recently occupied by the Van Garretts. Though Samuel Philipse professed no bitterness towards the loss of his family's status, Irving queried whether a man with such vested interests in the assets of Sleepy Hollow should be placed in charge of executing the Van Garrett estate.

Peter Van Garrett had left all of his worldly goods and property to his son, Dirk, who was killed soon afterwards by the Horseman. Dirk, being a relatively young man of only 30 years, and a bachelor, had made no will. As such, the deeds of the Van Garrett manor and lands were to be auctioned in Tarrytown. Every man and woman of Sleepy Hollow had some vested interest in this land sale, as half the town was still tenanted on the Van Garrett land, and a change in ownership amounted to uncertain futures for the long-time residents. Philipse, though of modest means, planned to bid at the auction himself, and Irving noted that the man had kept details of the auction as quiet as possible, so as to reduce the opposition to his claim. His primary rival, however, was surely Baltus Van Tassel, now the wealthiest man in Sleepy Hollow, and so it was to the Van Tassel home that Irving ventured next.

When Washington Irving arrived, he found the patriarch alone – Katrina and Brom had ventured to New York and would not be back until the following evening. When Irving entered the Van Tassel home he found it in a state of mourning for Baltus' dead wife; but despite the dreadful circumstances Baltus was not one to turn away cordial visitors, and extended Irving every hospitality. Baltus Van Tassel, though a man of considerable wealth, was also modest with it. He was in no way ostentatious, and all the residents of Sleepy Hollow agreed that he was a fine and generous fellow.

Through a combination of gentle prying and taking heed of the village gossip, Irving had learned that Van Tassel's late wife, Maria, had once been a commoner – a serving girl in the Van Tassel household. When Baltus had married her, Maria had been raised in status, earning her some jealousy from within the townstead, and some acrimony from Baltus' daughter, Katrina. Baltus maintained, however, that Maria and Katrina had eventually settled their differences, and had grown to care for one another as mother and daughter. That was, until recently.

Baltus reluctantly confessed that Maria had opposed the marriage of Katrina and Brom Bones, favoring instead the match between Katrina and the stranger, Ichabod Crane. Though Katrina thought Crane was most ill-aspected, Maria had insisted that he be allowed to court her stepdaughter, maintaining that a fine gentleman from the city would raise the family's fortunes in society. Baltus went along with his wife's thinking to please her, and confessed that Katrina had become most anguished as a result.

Katrina Van Brunt (nee Van Tassel) was a rare beauty, whose charms inadvertently led to the demise of the amorous Ichabod Crane.

A lightning-stricken tree of unusual size, this twisted, black tree is haunted by the ghost of Major André, and marks the bounds of the Horseman's territory.

Not wishing to cause Baltus further upset – and now suspecting that Katrina or Brom, or both, could be behind the Horseman's attacks – Irving returned to Sleepy Hollow to find out more about the Van Tassels and their relationship with Ichabod Crane.

His inquiries led him eventually to the Old Dutch Church, where the Reverend Steenwyck was preparing to close up for the evening. Steenwyck, a staunch man of the cloth of old Dutch heritage, was a judgmental sort, and Irving found that the clergyman had few kind words to say about the Van Tassel women, saying that both Maria and Katrina were superstitious maids who allowed their love of folklore, legends, and heathen charms to come between them and their Sunday worship on more than one occasion. The reverend also extended his scorn to Ichabod Crane, saying that:

> *Our man of letters was peculiarly happy in the smiles of all the country damsels. How he would figure among them in the church-yard … or sauntering, with a whole bevy of them, along the banks of the adjacent mill-pond; while the more bashful country bumpkins hung sheepishly back, envying his superior elegance and address.*

It seemed, therefore, that Crane had been something of a ladies' man, and that his professed love for Katrina might well have been nought but bluster. Although any young man in the village might thus have had cause to dislike Crane – nay, and the girls' fathers besides! – this again confirmed to Irving's mind that Katrina and Brom were prime suspects, until the Reverend Steenwyck added one curious afterthought.

"Of course," he said, "I informed Katrina's father of the young man's behavior at once. It would not do for a girl of fine breeding to be seen fraternizing with such an ungallant 'gentleman,' and he agreed. Perhaps it is for the best that he … *ahem* … left us so suddenly."

Irving stopped to ponder these words a while, as the good reverend left the church and made his way home. Perhaps, Irving thought, Baltus Van Tassel was not so innocent after all. If he had known of Crane's reputation, he would surely have opposed any suggestion that Katrina and Crane marry. How strongly had he and his wife disagreed on that subject, Irving mused? With his mind full of conspiracies, and nightfall now completely upon him, Irving mounted his horse and made for his home across the south side of the stream, shuddering when he remembered he would have to pass through Wiley Swamp, where Ichabod Crane had supposedly met a sticky end.

By the time his horse had plodded to the fringe of the dense grove, the sky had drawn black with cloud, barely allowing a sliver of moon to light the uneven trail. Irving hoped to meet a watchman en route, but there was no sound of another living soul to be heard, just the dull echo of his mount's hooves on the forest floor. Irving knew he had lingered too long in Sleepy Hollow, and urged the horse on faster, though he could barely see his way. Presently, he caught sight of a silvery light off to his right, which at first he took to be a marsh-light – a phenomenon he had heard of but never seen. Though he was wary of the tales of restless spirits he had heard since his arrival, Irving was a man of sound constitution and rational mind, and thus stopped to peer at the strange light. Through its luminescence, he realized that he was close to the site of an extraordinarily large, gnarled tulip tree, known locally as the "Tree of the Dead" or sometimes "the Hanging Tree," on account of the legend of Major André. The British major's execution was often mistakenly attributed to this part of Sleepy Hollow, where the ghost apparently still lingered. And with that thought in his mind, Irving gasped as the silvery light coalesced into a human form. Wisping through the trees was a man, in clothes long out of fashion, translucent and shimmering, with the twisted black outline of the hanging tree silhouetted behind him.

BROM BONES

Brom Bones was the hero of the scene, having come to the gathering on his favorite steed Daredevil, a creature, like himself, full of mettle and mischief, and which no one but himself could manage. He was, in fact, noted for preferring vicious animals, given to all kinds of tricks which kept the rider in constant risk of his neck, for he held a tractable, well-broken horse as unworthy of a lad of spirit.

Abraham Van Brunt, called Brom Bones, was a strong, broad-shouldered man – a rowdy and local hero. Famed for his horsemanship, his physical strength, and his love of tricks and merriment, Brom was "always ready for a fight or a frolic." He was the leader of a small band of men who looked up to him and with whom he rode throughout the countryside playing pranks and getting into brawls.

Ichabod Crane, in his journal, noted that Brom was ill-dispositioned towards him, resorting to insults and cheap tricks to remove the schoolmaster from Katrina Van Tassel's affections. The later disappearance of Crane was widely thought to have been at the hands of Brom, rather than the Horseman, though none could prove as much and Brom certainly would not admit to the crime.

Irving trembled at the thought of seeing a real ghost, but with grim fascination he leaned forward in the saddle and squinted to get a better look. As he did so, the floating figure changed direction, moving closer, and then gaining in speed. A loud moan filled Irving's ears, and the ghost of Major André rushed upon him like a rolling fog bank, ghastly face torn in an expression of pain, mouth gaping open impossibly widely. At this, Irving's horse reared and threw him, before galloping off into the night. Uninjured, Irving stood at once, full of terror, though he was quite alone – the spirit had dissipated like morning mist.

However, that was not the end of Irving's predicament. His heart had barely stopped racing when he heard another sound from behind him; the slow, steady clomp of hooves, accompanied by the deep, guttural breaths of a horse that has labored hard. Irving turned slowly, his hackles up. He saw nothing but darkness at first, but then small pinpricks of dancing yellow light moved about from further down the trail. They drew nearer, until soon Irving made out a faint orange glow of a jack o'lantern, shimmering off a sweat-slick horse. Hoof scraped stone, the horse snorted. Irving saw a dark outline of a black-clad horseman picking its way through the glade, and knew at once what followed him. The Headless Horseman was abroad!

Irving had no desire to wait and see if this was another prank of some local rowdy. He turned on his heels and, half-blind with the darkness, ran as fast as his legs would carry him in the direction of the log bridge that marked the edge of the Horseman's hunting grounds.

Irving was in the grip of terror. His heart pounded and his legs pumped to carry him away from danger, and yet he heard the gallop of the horse behind him, and ducked instinctively as a sword-blade swept through the air, aimed for the space where his neck had been a second earlier. Irving plunged into the undergrowth, hoping to slow the Horseman in the tangle of the forest, if indeed the Hessian was a substantial being at all. The snap of branches and the tearing of brambles came from behind, and Irving knew the Horseman came on still. He had only his walking cane to help him through the terrain, and it felt most inadequate. The scholar's feet slipped into marshy ground, water lapping over the collars of his shoes, and he feared he might inadvertently wade into the swamp and do the Horseman's grim work for him, when suddenly a silvered light appeared up ahead.

Irving cared no longer if the light was Major André's mournful spirit – he followed it, with the Horseman behind him all the way, until at last he plunged out onto the trail and, by the pale light of the moon that had so miraculously emerged from the thick clouds, Irving saw his own horse upon the path.

Abraham Van Brunt, a rowdy and local hero, long held as a suspect in the disappearance of Ichabod Crane.

He knew that if he hesitated the beast would bolt at the sight of the Horseman, and so he at once mounted his horse, turning it about and sending it into a gallop as the Hessian burst from the undergrowth, flaming pumpkin-head blazing in one hand and long sword held in the other. Irving threw caution to the wind, hurtling along the twisting trail with the Horseman close on his heels. Twice more he felt the swish of air as the Horseman slashed at him with his blade, and yet he escaped, and soon he saw the log bridge up ahead, which spurred him on doubly.

The Horseman gained on Irving, and began to draw alongside – his infernal steed was imbued with some preternatural vigor. But Irving was not done; he reached to his saddle and pulled out the heavy pistol that he often carried on his journeys north. The Horseman flailed at Irving again, but the scholar ducked beneath the sweeping blade, turned and fired.

The shot struck the Horseman square in the chest, striking him from the horse, which veered into the undergrowth with a whinny. Irving chanced a look back – suddenly fearful that he had slain a prankster from the village – only to see the black-clad Hessian sit bolt upright, and then stand, holding the jack o'lantern high to light his way as he began to follow on foot. No matter how fast Irving rode, the Hessian always seemed to be a few steps behind, walking with menace, sword slicing the air with the promise of violence. Yet, finally, Irving saw the log bridge ahead, and hurtled across it just as Ichabod Crane had done on that fateful night. Safely across at last, he pulled up his mount and turned to see the Headless Horseman, seemingly unable to set foot on the bridge. The Hessian paced back and forth, pointing his blade at Irving, until finally his horse cantered to his side, misty breath snorting from its nostrils. The Horseman mounted his devilish steed, and turned once more, holding the jack o'lantern aloft and hurling it at Irving with uncanny force.

Irving, being cut from a bolder cloth than his predecessor, had expected this. He already had his walking cane in hand, and batted away the pumpkin with all his might. Still, the force of the impact rattled him, and almost unseated him; his cane burst into flames and instantly became so hot that Irving was forced to drop it. But he remained in the saddle, and nodded defiantly to his pursuer. At that, the Hessian reared up on his horse, and vanished into the night like shadows before the dawn.

Summoning and Vanquishing the Horseman

So it was that Washington Irving came to realize without a doubt that the Headless Horseman was being controlled by mortals for their own nefarious purposes. What's more, now he was almost certain who was to blame.

Irving woke after a fitful sleep of nightmares and fever-dreams. He was shaken, but alive. Irving refused to be chased from Sleepy Hollow before his work was done, and turned once more to Crane's books. Within them,

Irving discovered a variety of charms to ward off evil spirits, and to summon them. The former were employed at once, to provide a safe haven for Irving's investigation. The latter were studied closely, for ideas as to his next recourse.

According to Crane's notes, whoever controlled the Horseman must possess the head, and it would have to be kept somewhere warded against the Horseman's powers. The church was certainly the most obvious place, although it was small, possessing no crypt, and Irving could not see such a grisly trophy being hidden from the pious eyes of the Reverend Steenwyck. No, Irving recalled an earlier conversation regarding Katrina and Maria Van Tassel, in which they'd been accused of superstition and the making of "heathen charms"; witchcraft, perhaps, ran in the family. It was to the Van Tassel estate that Irving would go, and he must do so in broad daylight, when the creatures of the night held no power over the mortal realm. Crane's notes suggested that to end the Horseman's reign the head must be returned to the Hessian, or else buried with his body. Irving had only guesswork to tell him where the body might be, and did not much fancy the prospect of facing the Horseman again – thus he told himself he must take one step at a time. Firstly, he must find the head – then he could decide what to do with it.

The surrogate head carried by the Horseman appeared to be a jack o'lantern, though Irving believed it to be imbued with the very fires of hell.

(Previous spread)
"His terror rose to desperation; he rained a shower of kicks and blows upon Gunpowder, hoping by a sudden movement to give his companion the slip; but the specter started full jump with him. Away, then, they dashed through thick and thin; stones flying and sparks flashing at every bound."
– The Legend of Sleepy Hollow

It took some time before Irving had sufficiently calmed his nerves to return along the trail through Wiley Swamp. The area was ill-aspected even by day, but with no sign of ghostly activity Irving was able to reach Sleepy Hollow unmolested.

Irving ensconced himself within the hayloft of an old barn on the Van Tassel estate, within view of the house and outlying buildings, and kept watch. Many hours passed, with Baltus rarely leaving the house except to send some servant or other running to his duties. Eventually, however, as Irving had lost all feeling in his limbs and had almost dozed off, he saw Baltus leaving the house, acting in a most furtive manner. Alarmingly, the old patriarch headed straight for the barn, which Irving had presumed disused, and entered.

Through the cracks in the floorboards, Irving spied on Baltus, who set about moving several sacks and crates, uncovering at last a large trapdoor. Irving held his breath as he watched Baltus take up a lantern and move down into the concealed cellar. He was gone perhaps half an hour before returning, carefully replacing every item before extinguishing the lantern and leaving the barn.

A woodsman's axe, like the one purportedly used by the Hessian to decapitate Dirk Van Garrett.

Almost at once, Irving climbed down from the hayloft and embarked upon uncovering the cellar door. Taking up Baltus' lantern, he moved down a set of rough-hewn steps and followed a tight corridor until he reached a small chamber. Irving imagined that this would have provided some safe haven during the war, although that was far from its purpose now. The walls and floor were painted with sigils and strange script, reminiscent of those from Crane's journal. In the center of the room stood a small plinth, upon which was a filthy cloth bundle and a large, leather-bound book. Even before unwrapping the bundle, Irving knew what he would find, and he was quickly proved correct – a human skull, grinning and dark with age. The book was bound about with straps, and sealed with an iron lock, though Irving recognized it as a magical *grimoire*. How it had come into the possession of Baltus Van Tassel he knew not, though he supposed madness and wealth made it possible to procure any exotic item, should a man wish it. With little time remaining until dusk, Irving bundled the grimoire with the skull, and beat a hasty retreat.

In his eagerness to leave the estate, however, Irving failed to notice a servant of the Van Tassels loading a wagon near to the barn. Stealing away in the waning light, he was sighted by the laborer and the alarm was quickly raised. As Irving reached his horse, he heard a commotion from the house behind him, as Baltus Van Tassel summoned his men to give chase. Whether or not he had been identified Irving did not know, but he had the head and the book – if he could only evade capture and return to his house before nightfall, he could yet lay the spirit of the Hessian to rest once and for all. With this in mind, he galloped away as fast as his horse was able.

Irving was not the most accomplished horseman, and before long he heard the sound of Baltus' men gaining on him. By the time he reached Wiley Swamp, they had almost drawn level, and Irving recognized some of the men as Brom Bones' old gang – a posse not to be trifled with. When one of them drew a pistol and shouted for Irving to pull up, he had little choice but to oblige, but not before cantering to the clearing by the Tree of the Dead, for Irving had a notion that he could still wrest victory for the situation in that haunted place.

When he came to a stop, however, in the darkening grove, the rowdies set upon him, dragging the young scholar from his horse and roughhousing him until he gave up the stolen bundle. They held him there for what seemed like an age, until the sound of a pony and trap could be heard coming to a halt on the path through the trees, and soon Baltus Van Tassel himself traipsed through the undergrowth and into the clearing. The old man's eyes were afire with menace.

"So," said he, "another supposed 'gentleman' comes to take what is mine, like a thief in the night. Though I must say I am surprised to see you again, young Master Irving."

"Surprised?" said Irving, defiantly. "Because you thought your Hessian had ended me last night?"

This brought nervous laughter from Van Tassel's ruffians, who perhaps did not believe in ghosts and goblins. Van Tassel smirked, and held out a hand, into which one of his men pressed the bundle of rags.

"It matters not what you believe, Mr Irving. All that matters is that I have my property back safe and sound, and your time in Sleepy Hollow is at an end. I trust I don't have to warn you to go back to New York and never return?"

Before anyone could reply, the snapping of a twig reverberated around the clearing, and the temperature dropped to a chilling degree. The leaves upon the forest floor scattered as a sudden breeze picked up, and before the eyes of the assembled men appeared a mist-like form – the silvery phantom of Major André – moaning and rushing to and fro. This was enough to break the nerve of the simple rowdies, who fled for their horses and raced away as the ghostly wails intensified. Irving seized his moment, snatching the Hessian's skull from where he'd hidden it in his saddlebag. Baltus, realizing that the bundle he held did not contain the skull at all, fired his pistol, causing Irving's horse to bolt. Now without a steed and with night drawing in, Irving dashed to the Tree of the Dead for cover as Baltus drew a second pistol and gave chase.

A Final Confrontation

The night grew darker and darker; the stars seemed to sink deeper in the sky, and driving clouds occasionally hid them from his sight. He had never felt so lonely and dismal. He was, moreover, approaching the very place where many of the scenes of the ghost stories had been laid. In the center of the road stood an enormous tulip-tree, which towered like a giant above all the other trees of the neighborhood, and formed a kind of landmark. Its limbs were gnarled and fantastic, large enough to form trunks for ordinary trees, twisting down almost to the earth, and rising again into the air.

It was only a matter of time before the patriarch caught up with Irving, and pointed the pistol at the young scholar.

"Hand me the skull!" he snapped. "Or it will be the end of you."

Irving held the skull out towards the marsh. "Hold your fire, Baltus, or I'll throw it into the marsh – perhaps you'll find it before the Hessian comes, but more likely you will not. And what will happen then, I wonder?"

"You'd be a fool to do it!" cried Baltus Van Tassel. "Without me to control the Horseman, who knows what he will do? You'll damn us both."

"I will have a confession from you first, Van Tassel. Why did you do it? Why kill those poor people in such a way?"

"Pah! Why else, foolish boy, but to secure my legacy. You would not understand. Everything I have done, I have done for my daughter, and the continued prosperity of my line. The Van Garretts deserved all they got – lording it over the good people of this village for years, when they had only bought their way to title and power. The old families of this district deserve to have their time again – the

Van Tassels, Steenwycks, and Van Brunts. I secured the Van Garrett estate as my daughter's dowry, though my wife insisted that Katrina set up home there with the odious Ichabod Crane. I could not allow such a thing, not after I learned what he was about. The Reverend Steenwyck hoped that I would let him buy the manor rather than see it in the hands of that philanderer, but I had a better plan. With Crane gone, Brom could wed Katrina, and two of the oldest families in Sleepy Hollow would be united. Yet my wife still opposed the match, and what's more she discovered what I had done. She'd always had the touch of the witch about her, that one. Though I regret her death the most, when she threatened to expose my secret to Katrina in order to sabotage the engagement, I had to act quickly; a fine coincidence that it threw the suspicion away from my house."

As Baltus reveled in his own cleverness, night drew in completely, and the patriarch failed to notice the drop in temperature and rising mists that presaged the coming of something unnatural. He primed his pistol to fire, when he saw the strange look in Irving's eyes, and heard a heavy footfall behind him. The Horseman had arrived.

"It matters not, Irving!" shouted Baltus. "The Hessian obeys his last instruction still – and he comes for you!"

THE OLD DUTCH CHURCH

The sequestered situation of this church seems always to have made it a favorite haunt of troubled spirits... On one side of the church extends a wide woody dell, along which raves a large brook among broken rocks and trunks of fallen trees. Over a deep black part of the stream was formerly thrown a wooden bridge; the road that led to it, and the bridge itself, were thickly shaded by overhanging trees, which cast a gloom about it, even in the daytime; but occasioned a fearful darkness at night. Such was one of the favorite haunts of the Headless Horseman, and the place where he was most frequently encountered.

The local church, known simply as "the Old Dutch Church," is a 17th-century stone building, which sits within a five-acre churchyard. Its borders are not marked, and roll into the contiguous Sleepy Hollow Cemetery, and probably merge into long-forgotten Indian burial grounds too. The old families of Sleepy Hollow lie here, alongside the dead of the Battle of White Plains, some in mass or unmarked graves. The church was built by Fredrick Philipse I as a place of worship for the tenants of his manor, which later became the settlement of Sleepy Hollow.

Some say that the Hessian's body lies within the churchyard; even so, the Headless Horseman cannot enter the sanctified ground – his dark horse shies away from the invisible barrier around the perimeter as though there is a solid wall before it.

The Hessian rode forward menacingly, his old uniform now almost entirely black and tattered, his high-collared cloak hiding the grievous wound at his neck.

"I think not, Van Tassel," replied Irving. "Your devilry ends tonight!" With that, he threw the skull with all his might, and dived to the ground as Baltus discharged his pistol, the leaden shot striking a tree across the marsh.

Baltus could only look on in horror as the Horseman snatched the skull from the air, and squeezed it onto his neck. The grinning skull turned to Van Tassel, eyes now blazing with hellfire, and in that moment the old man dropped to the ground, his wits deserting him. He whimpered like a small child, begging for mercy, although the Horseman seemed not to notice he was even there. The Hessian strode past Van Tassel, mounted his steed, and in a flash of smoke and lightning was gone from this Earth, forevermore.

Irving requisitioned Van Tassel's trap, and drove the defeated villain back to the village. Baltus had been driven quite mad by the experience, and was never able to speak sense of what had happened. Knowing that no-one would believe the truth, Irving simply told the militia that he had found the old man out by Wiley Swamp when he was returning home – none of the rowdies ever confessed to their part in the matter, nor to how they had been frightened by a ghost whilst threatening an innocent man.

The churchyard outside the famous Old Dutch Church of Sleepy Hollow, said to be the final resting place of the Hessian's remains.

By the time Irving returned to New York, the Reverend Steenwyck had purchased his old family pile, and Katrina and Brom took ownership of the Van Tassel estate. The grimoire, however, was removed from Sleepy Hollow by Irving, to be secreted in the secret library of the Lycean, where it remains still …

Irving's Occult Studies

Believing the Horseman to be defeated, Washington Irving wrote about the exploits of Ichabod Crane in the form of a fictional, yet cautionary, tale. When its publication found some international success, he was able to devote the coming years to his studies into the occult, delving into ancient folklore and magical texts, and forming strong ties with several notable psychical detection organizations around the globe. He was endlessly fascinated by the legends of headless horsemen in particular, knowing how deadly they could be to the unwary.

Irving investigated several American headless hauntings, before venturing to Europe for several years, where he hoped to find the source of the strange phenomena. He journeyed to England, France, and Germany, uncovering – and even successfully defeating at times – dark forces, continuing the Lycean Club's secret war against dangerous supernatural entities.

When at last he returned to the United States in 1835, Irving built a home on the bounds of Sleepy Hollow, which he called Sunnyside in honor of his final victory over the darkness that Van Tassel had wrought.

Chapter 3 - Headless Horsemen through History

Though the *Legend of Sleepy Hollow* has remained the most enduring and famous tale of headless horsemen, Irving's research revealed to him that decollated spirits have roamed the earth since ancient times. In each case they appear to be earthbound due to some great wrong that has befallen them, and almost always presage some terrible disaster or death if they are seen by mortals. Some are said to appear randomly, forewarning of the imminent death of the unfortunate observer. Others seem to be driven by a sinister force, appearing quite deliberately in order to bring about the end of an unwitting victim for reasons unknown. That these spirits were more powerful and of greater sentience than other mournful ghosts was beyond question to the young Irving. What made them especially dangerous, however, was that they could be controlled, as he knew from bitter experience. Thus, he sought to study the strange phenomenon of headless horsemen; to catalog and document their appearances worldwide, in the hope that he could better understand – and one day defeat – this terrible race of revenants.

Irving travelled first to England, ostensibly to pursue his writing career at the behest of his friend Walter Scott. Initially he had hoped to travel to Germany, and perhaps even to meet the Grimms, but in the end he remained for a while in the industrial city of Birmingham with relatives while he worked on his books. The real reason for the delay, of course, was that he had found in the British Isles more tales of headless spirits than he had ever dreamt of, and so he visited London and Edinburgh frequently to delve into tales far older than he had expected.

English Horsemen

Irving had not expected England to be so steeped in legends of headless ghosts, giants, horsemen, and beasts. Indeed, the more time he spent poring over old books of folklore, the more he started to believe that the headless spirits he sought had not originated in Germany at all, but in Britain. Of course, Britain had been invaded many times over its long history, and so many of its traditions had come from far-off lands, from Scandinavia and continental Europe to the holy lands of the Middle East. Yet the British Isles were littered with ancient sites of undeniable esoteric power – Avebury, Salisbury, Tintagel, Ballymeanoch, and Bennachie amongst others – and Irving began to believe that the ancient magic that the Britons of old had believed in was somehow giving power to the headless phantoms that had arrived here with superstitious invaders many centuries earlier.

Irving's interest in British legends was truly piqued when he was travelling by coach one day from Birmingham to the picturesque walled city of Chester. Along the road he stopped at a low-rent coaching inn near the village of Duddon, of some considerable age, named The Headless Woman. Such a name was not uncommon, Irving learned, but he soon found that the name of this particular establishment had its own eerie legend attached. The name of the public house recalled the tale of a serving girl – one Grace Trigg – from the nearby Hockenhull Hall, who had died a violent death in 1664. Local legend went that she had been found hiding in a cellar by Cromwell's parliamentarian soldiers after the hall's owners – outspoken royalists – had fled. The girl was tortured in the inn to give up

One of the most haunted public houses in Britain, in the Cheshire village of Duddon, plagued by the headless ghost of the murdered Grace Trigg.

the location of the family's hidden valuables, but would not say. For her loyalty, she was dragged upstairs to the attic and beheaded; her body was later dumped in the River Gowy. Over the years many locals have reported seeing the headless spirit of Grace Trigg during periods of disquiet – she supposedly crawls out of the river with her head under her arm, walks through the maize fields that bound the village, and returns to the inn's attic, where she wails and cries the night through. Anyone who sees her on her wanderings is sure to lose a blood relative soon, or else to be betrayed in some heinous fashion.

Upon hearing this story, Irving secured rooms for the night and, against the advice of the innkeeper, insisted on staying in the attic. Using his books from the New York Lycean, he cast about his bed a circle of protection, and spent the night in silent vigil. He was only partly disappointed – although no apparition appeared before him, he did hear a quiet sobbing from the

Black Shuck – an infamous demonic hound of England – sometimes appears headless, yet still howling. His appearance presages the death of any who witness him.

corner of the attic room, which filled him with great melancholy. When the sobbing stopped, Irving – remembering his last encounter with a headless spirit – lit his lantern and ventured from his circle. In the far corner of the room, he was horrified to discover a pool of dark blood, seeping across the floorboards. Irving retreated back to his bed at once, and spent a restless night. The next morning, the landlord informed Irving that the blood stain often appeared, especially at night, and no amount of scrubbing would remove it.

The interlude was a strange one, but it led to further delving into Britain's folklore. Once Irving's business in Chester was complete, he spent some time in London at the original Lycean Club. Welcomed as an American member of the elite club, Irving spent much time in the library, which was packed full of esoteric writings. There he learned of the Black Shucks – ghostly dogs that supposedly roam rural England and whose appearance precedes tragedy. Oftentimes the great black hounds have no heads, and yet manage to howl all the same, their chilling calls echoing across windswept moors across England, from Dartmoor to York. He read of the myriad headless ghosts of England who, like Grace Trigg, seem earthbound and set on some purpose that is unfathomable to men. From Anne Boleyn to Sir Walter Raleigh, these spirits most often wander great ancestral piles, as if somehow royal blood imbues them with particular unearthly vigor.

Of these spirits, Irving was particularly fascinated by the ghosts of Oxford. At St. John's College within the famous university, the Archbishop William Laud was said to haunt the library, kicking his head around the aisles at night. Much like Grace Trigg, Laud was also beheaded by parliamentarian forces, and Irving theorized that strong religious beliefs might have lent his wronged spirit considerable power. The same could be said for the other frequent haunt of Oxford – a man named Napier – who was hung, drawn, and quartered in 1610 for his Catholic beliefs. A martyr, his ghost apparently "pulled himself together," all but for the head, which was never found. Napier's purpose for staying in the mortal realm is almost certainly revenge – Irving found that many good Protestants had died of mysterious illnesses or fatal accidents after reporting a sighting of the headless ghost.

Irving lost himself in his studies, but swiftly realized that mere ghost stories could be found the world over. What he needed to do while in Britain was to look for the source of the stories – the legends and myths that preceded all tales of haunted houses. And while on the shores of fabled Albion, there was but one place to begin: the tales of King Arthur.

THE HEADLESS GHOSTS OF BLICKLING HALL

A grand Jacobean country house in Norfolk, Blickling Hall boasts one of the largest collections of headless ghost legends in all England, and is visited frequently by the decollated spirit of none other than Anne Boleyn, Henry VIII's second wife, who lived there as a girl.

Spectral activity began at Blickling Hall when news of Anne's death reached Norfolk in the spring of 1536. Across the countryside, many reported seeing four headless horses dragging the body of a headless man. The apparition crossed 12 bridges in a single night, before ending its haunt within the grounds of Blickling Hall. In the months that followed two separate spirits began to be sighted around the house and grounds, and more would follow. The first is the Grey Lady – thought by some to be Anne – who regularly strolls by the lake and has been seen in the house. Unusually for most ghosts, she has on occasion interacted with people, responding to questions, often with the phrase "That for which I search is lost forever." The second ghost, which is very much confirmed to be the spirit of Anne Boleyn, is a headless spirit who carried her head around the halls of the house, dripping blood as she goes. This is a terrifying sight, though there has been no recorded incident of the apparition bringing any calamity upon the household. That cannot be said, however, of the ghostly carriage that bears Anne to Blickling. On the anniversary of her execution each year (May 19), Anne arrives at Blickling Hall in a carriage pulled by headless horses. It can be seen across the south of England from London to Norfolk, and woe betide any man of cruel heart or inconstant lover that sees it. Though Anne's ghost is doomed to repeat the same sequence of events each year, she seems to have some measure of control over her wanderings – she appears at various royal residences seemingly at random, and has a good many legends attached to her.

Several years after Anne's death, her father, Thomas, also died, and returned to Blickling Hall to haunt his former home. He engineered his daughter's marriage to England's monarch, and lost his daughter and his son as a result. As penance he is required to cross a dozen bridges before the cock crows each day for a thousand years. His route takes him from Blickling to Wroxham, and he is sighted at many villages in between. Just like his daughter, Thomas carries his head under his arms, but rather than ooze blood, his mouth gushes flames, perhaps symbolizing the torment he suffers.

(OPPOSITE)
One of the most famous headless spirits in England, Anne Boleyn's ghost is said to wander between several locales, notably the Tower of London, Blickling Hall, and Windsor Castle.

Sir Gawain and the Green Knight

(OPPOSITE)
Archbishop William Laud, who haunts the library of St John's College in Oxford.

With a rough rasping the reins he twists,
hurled out the hall door, his head in his hand,
that the fire of the flint flew from fleet hooves.
to what land he came no man there knew,
no more than they knew where he had come from
what then?
The king and Gawain there
at that green man laugh and grin;
yet broadcast it was abroad
as a marvel among those men.

One of the oldest tales of headless horsemen to exist in the library of the Lycean Club was the tale of Sir Gawain and the Green Knight. The oldest known manuscript – a copy of which Irving studied at length while in London – is believed to date from the late 14th century, written by an unknown scholar. The origin of the tale, steeped as it is in Celtic faerie-lore, is certainly older still, and Irving felt sure that he had found one of the first known records of headless spirits interacting with mortal men. The tale recounts how, during a New Year's Eve feast at King Arthur's court, the Green Knight paid an unexpected visit to Camelot. He challenged Arthur to strike him with his own axe, on the condition that the king agreed to receive a blow in return exactly one year and a day hence.

Arthur hesitated, but when the Green Knight mocked his reticence, the king stepped forward. At this, Sir Gawain leapt up and asked to take on the challenge himself as the king's champion. Once given leave to do so, Gawain took hold of the Green Knight's axe and, in one deadly blow, cut off the knight's head. To the amazement of the court, the decapitated knight picked up his severed head and, before riding away, reiterated the terms of the pact – the young Gawain must seek him in a year and a day at the Green Chapel to receive the return strike.

Time passed, and autumn arrived. On the Day of All Saints, Gawain prepared to leave Camelot and find the Green Knight. Putting on his best armor, he mounted his horse, Gringolet, and set off through the wilderness. Upon his journey, Gawain encountered all manner of beasts, suffered from hunger and cold, and grew increasingly desperate. On Christmas Day, Gawain prayed to find a place to hear Mass, and looked up to see a castle in the distance. The lord of the castle, Bertilak, welcomed Gawain warmly, introducing him to his lady and a strange old woman who sat beside her, never speaking. For sport, Bertilak struck a deal with Gawain: the host would go out hunting with his men each day, and when he returned in the evening, he would exchange his winnings for anything Gawain has managed

to acquire by staying behind at the castle.

The first day, the lord hunted a herd of does while Gawain slept late. That morning, the lord's wife crept into Gawain's chambers and attempted to seduce him. Gawain refused her, but before she left she stole one kiss from him. That evening, when the host gave Gawain the venison he had caught, Gawain kissed him, since he had won one kiss from the lady. The second day, the lord hunted a wild boar; the lady again entered Gawain's chambers, and this time kissed him twice. That evening Gawain gave the host the two kisses in exchange for the boar's head. The third day, the lord hunted a fox, and the lady kissed Gawain three times. She also offered Gawain her girdle, as a token of her love. The green silk girdle around her waist was no ordinary cloth, she claimed, but was possessed of the magical ability to protect the wearer from death. Intrigued, Gawain accepted the cloth, but when it came to the time to exchange his winnings with the host, Gawain gave the three kisses but did not mention the lady's green girdle. The host gave Gawain the fox skin he had won that day, seemingly none the wiser.

When New Year's Day arrived, Gawain donned his armor and the girdle and set out for the Green Chapel. Eventually, he came to a narrow defile in a rock face. He heard sounds of life and, believing the Green Chapel to be near, Gawain called out. Sure enough, the Green Knight emerged to greet him. Intent on fulfilling the terms of the contract, Gawain presented his neck to the Green Knight, who proceeded to feign two blows, with the intent of making Gawain flinch, and thus besmirch his honor. On the third feint, the Green Knight nicked Gawain's neck, only barely drawing blood. Angered, Gawain shouted that the contract had been met, and at this the Green Knight merely laughed.

The Green Knight revealed himself to be Bertilak, lord of the castle where Gawain had sheltered. Because Gawain had not honestly exchanged all of his winnings on the third day, Bertilak had drawn blood on his third blow. Nevertheless, Gawain had proven himself a worthy knight, without equal in all the land. Bertilak explained that the old woman who accompanied his wife at the castle was really Morgan le Faye, King Arthur's half-sister. She had sent the Green Knight on his errand to Camelot, and used her magic to change Bertilak's appearance. Gawain returned to Arthur's court, relieved to be alive, but ashamed that he had not been truthful about the girdle. As penance, he tied it around his arm and wore it always. However, the other knights of the Round Table, believing Gawain's honor to be intact, followed suit, wearing girdles about their arms to show their support.

For Washington Irving, the story was deeply meaningful. He had read many times of myths regarding "the wild hunt," which Bertilak surely represented. In addition, Irving saw the role of Morgan le Faye as a cautionary note regarding the man or woman who controls the Headless Horseman. In

(OPPOSITE)
Sir Gawain and the Green Knight
Transformed by Morgan le Faye, the Green Knight is able to withstand his beheading at the hands of the knight Gawain, and returns a year to the day in order to test Gawain's valor. Had Gawain lacked sufficient mettle, Morgana's dark magic would surely have claimed his life.

this case, the knight was driven to a purpose: whether trickery or deceit, or a genuine attempt to claim the life of Arthur, who could tell. What Irving supposed was that headless spirits were bound by supernatural laws that could be exploited by a wily occultist, and that their very existence was a sort of pact with unseen forces. Irving began to suspect that headless spirits were not spirits at all in the traditional sense, but supernatural entities from some other realm entirely. What the superstitious people of the British Isles might call "fairy-folk" or "fae," and what more god-fearing men might call demons.

Celtic Horsemen

Legends of the fairy-folk would enter Irving's research for the rest of his time in Great Britain. In Wales, where the story of the Green Knight probably originated, he heard many obscure tales of headless ghosts: Lady Matthias of Stackpole who roams her estate in a coach pulled by headless horses and driven by a headless coachman; a similar headless lady pulled by a near-identical team of horses in Tenby, supposedly vanishing in a ball of fire if they're seen; and the ghost of Princess Gwenllian, the last Celtic warrior princess, beheaded in battle and consigned to roam the battlefield searching for her missing head. These were familiar tales, but did nothing to expand Irving's knowledge of the entities he hunted.

More promise was evident, however, when he visited Scotland and Ireland. In Scotland he heard tell of a legendary chieftain who held more than one similarity with the fearsome Hessian. In Ireland, on the other hand, Irving found several superstitious old sops who were more than willing to tell him tales of the fairy-folk and their great mischief. They perhaps thought Irving would take them for fools, but instead he used their stories to fuel further research, and before he was done in Ireland, he had found evidence of at least one powerful entity, which he had no desire to meet in person.

The Dullahan and the Gan Ceann

It was never fully clear to Irving whether the *Dullahan* and the *Gan Ceann* were the same entity by different names, or two separate creatures altogether. There were many similarities between the two, certainly, and Irving doubted that such terrible characteristics could be shared, and so he put the confusion down to local variance in mythology.

The Dullahan, as far as Irving could gather, was one of the Unseelie – a race of malevolent fairies. Whereas their opposite number – the Seelie – are prone to bouts of mischief, they rarely plague humans unless some slight has been perceived against them. The Unseelie, however, bring their assaults wherever they please – across Ireland peasants whisper of "Unseelie hosts" who will waylay lone travelers at night, lifting them into the air, beating them, and compelling them to commit heinous acts against their will. Most feared of all the Unseelie, the Dullahan is a bringer of dismay and death.

The Dullahan is a headless rider, clad in a flowing black cape and usually mounted upon a black horse that spews flames from its nostrils (this fiery connection, shared by the Dullahan, the Hessian's jack o'lantern and the ghost of Thomas Boleyn, set Irving to thinking of a more literal, hellish explanation for headless spirits). Sometimes, the entity instead drives a team of headless horses, drawing a ghostly black carriage adorned with funereal objects behind him, the sparking wheels setting hedgerows aflame as he passes. The Dullahan carries its rotting head aloft in one hand like a lantern, the better to see immense distances, while it holds a whip made from a human spinal cord in the other. As the specter gallops across the Irish countryside, gates and doors fly open at his approach, for nothing can impede the Dullahan's passage until his grim work is done. Mortals who see the Dullahan riding are often struck blind by the creature's hideous whip, or else are drenched in blood that splashes upwards from the horse's hooves. When the Dullahan finally draws to a halt, someone nearby will die, for the creature is a harbinger of death.

Unlike the Banshee, which warns families of a loved one's imminent death, the Dullahan is said to claim souls for himself, choosing his victims deliberately for some unknown reason. The only defense against this dreadful Unseelie is gold – Irving heard of a man from Galway who had tried to outrun the Dullahan but, when he realized there was no escaping his dread fate, he remembered that he had an old lucky gold coin in his pocket. He threw the coin on the road before the Dullahan, and the spirit roared in anger and vanished at once.

Ensconced within a library in Dublin, Irving found a legend about the Celtic fertility god, Crom Dubh, who was worshipped by an ancient king named Tighermas. Each year, Tighermas would sacrifice humans to Crom Dubh in exchange for his blessings, but all of that changed when the Christians came to Ireland. Like so many of the old gods, Crom Dubh was abandoned by his followers, but he was vengeful and would not be forgotten. He took the decaying form of the Dullahan, and now sets forth across the land on ancient feast days, when the veil between worlds is thin.

Irving felt sure that there was a strong connection between this strange Unseelie and the Hessian of Sleepy Hollow. Upon returning to Scotland, he put this theory forward to Walter Scott, who at once handed him a manuscript of one of his early works, entitled *The Wild Huntsman*. This story was translated from an older story by the German poet Gottfried August Bürger called *Der Wilde Jäger*. This story also featured headless spirits, which may, Scott postulated, have been part of the Germanic courts of elves – the Dökkálfar and Ljósálfar – almost certainly analogous to the Seelie and Unseelie of Celtic mythology. These tales would almost certainly have been known to the Dutch as early as the 16th century, and would thus have been carried across the sea to the American colonies, and to Sleepy Hollow. The evidence was mounting

Dullahan on chariot
The *Dullahan* is a headless fairy, who rides atop a carriage pulled by a black, headless horse. The creature has a whip made from the spine of a human corpse, and it is said that when the *Dullahan* stops riding a death occurs soon after. If one's name is called by the *Dullahan*, then death is instantaneous.

(OPPOSITE)
Ewan the Headless, clan chieftain, decapitated while making a last stand on the Isle of Mull. His spirit still rides about the island on the back of a headless horse, to warn of impending tragedy, or to claim the souls of his enemies' descendants.

THE CHIEFTAIN OF GLEN CAINNIR

The most famous headless spirit of Scotland has a more traditional explanation for its ghostly appearance.

In 1500 much of the southern parts of the Isle of Mull belonged to two factions of the Clan Maclaine, the Lochbuie and the Duart. In 1538, Ewan of the Little Head decided to dispose of his father, Iain Maclaine, and claim the castle of Mull for himself. Iain Maclaine, being in poor health, called on the Duart Maclaines to help him. The two factions met at Glen Cainnir, falling upon each other with axe and claymore. The fight went badly for Ewan's outnumbered clansmen, but he saw the Duart chieftain ahead of him and saw a way to end the battle at a stroke. Ewan drove his horse straight at the Duart leader, but was blindsided by an enemy clansman who, with a single blow, decapitated him.

Legend has it that Ewan's headless body flailed left and right, wounding several foes, before his horse bolted, carrying the upright body of its master all the way home. This was seen as a terrible omen, and the battle ended at once.

Upon returning to Loch Squabhain, Ewan's servants examined their lord's body – sure enough, the head was missing, even though the body still sat upright in the saddle, and twitched most disturbingly. A superstitious lot, they believed the devil must surely be at work, and thought perhaps that Ewan's horse was the source of the evil. To be sure, they decapitated the beast, before burying their lord.

Within a short space of time, Maclaine clansmen reported hearing the sound of ghostly hoof beats at night. Soon, the phenomenon stretched to the outlying villages, until at last the ghost of Ewan Maclaine was sighted several times. What set this restless spirit aside from other ghosts – for the Highlands are filled with such tales – was that whenever the ghost of Ewan Maclaine was seen, the witness would soon after die. Thus the strange thread of circumstance that links the appearance of headless revenants across the world was continued.

– Irving knew he would have to continue his European tour, and pay a visit soon to Germany. From that day, however, Washington Irving never traveled without his watch-chain of fine gold – just in case.

Germanic Horsemen

Washington Irving spent much of 1821 traveling in Europe, spending considerable time in Germany where he researched the old Germanic tales of headless spirits that the Dutch had perhaps taken with them to Sleepy Hollow. That the Hessian himself had been German served to confirm in Irving's mind that the root of these evil spirits lay in this European land.

(OPPOSITE)
The Grey Horseman
Supposedly the cursed spirit of a man who committed a crime punishable by decapitation, but who escaped his fate, the headless Grey Horseman is a persistent figure in the German backwoods. When he is encountered, he may "blow" his horn, signaling that the witness is fated to die.

Irving's mind flashed back to the tales of the Dullahan that he had heard in Ireland, and of the many legends of the "Death Coach" that often accompanied the appearance of that creature. The origins of phantom coaches could clearly be traced to the *Herlething* (Wild Hunt) of Germany, as well as to the ominous "*hell waine*," a wagon that carried off the souls of the damned, recorded by Reginald Scot in *The Discoverie of Witchcraft* (1584).

The Grey Horseman

Irving again returned to the Books of Grimm. Delving into the origins of a story called *Hans Jagendteufel* (Jack the Hunting-Devil), Irving found a succinct reasoning for the existence of headless horsemen. Relating events supposed to have taken place in 1644, the Grimms wrote: "It is believed that if a man commits a crime punishable by decapitation and it remains undiscovered during his lifetime, he will have to wander around after his death with his head under his arm."

Hans Jagendteufel describes how a young woman from Dresden was out gathering acorns in the forest, near to a place called Lost Waters. She was interrupted by a loud blast from a hunting horn. She turned to see a headless man in a long grey coat sitting on a grey horse. The apparition wore high boots and spurs, and carried a hunting horn. Fortunately for her, on this occasion, the headless rider passed on without doing her any harm, but she knew from the legends that she'd had a lucky escape. In some versions of the tale, the Grey Huntsman seeks out the perpetrators of capital crimes, taking their lives in much the same way as the Hessian did back in Sleepy Hollow. In others, he is accompanied by a pack of black hunting hounds with tongues of fire. This final reference chilled Irving to the bone – again he had seen mention of "hell fire," and again he wondered if he had seen exactly that back home. There was some dark magic involved in the legends of the headless horsemen, of that Irving was sure. The early Christians had labeled these revenants devils, but as he had seen in Ireland, there was surely older, pagan belief at the root.

Finding his membership of the Lycean Club to open doors, Irving visited the University of Marburg, and finally met the Brothers Grimm. They were not quite as he had expected – being of modest means and coming from a family of small income, the brothers were not allowed to be a full part of the university, though they lived and studied there and had enjoyed great success. Instead they were consigned to meager quarters on the edge of the university grounds, where they made Irving their honored guest. There, in a draughty library, he was introduced to the original Books of Grimm, and spent many hours poring over them, with the help of the brothers themselves, who lent him every assistance with the translation of their work. It was there that Irving found the missing pieces of the puzzle.

The Horseman of the Wild Hunt, like many headless revenants across the world, is not strictly speaking a ghost, but a cursed individual "scorned by God and cast from His light," usually for committing some heinous sin or act of blasphemy. Forced to wander in a twilight world betwixt heaven and hell, between life and death, the revenants can be set to work for whatever dark purpose is desired, by those who know how to control them. With the correct incantations and symbology, perfected in the 16th century by Dr John Dee of England, a horseman can be commanded to do the bidding of a mortal master, so long as that master has in his possession the remains of the horseman's head. Headless horsemen, it seemed, are capable of tearing the very soul from a mortal's body, or simply inflicting grievous harm in the traditional fashion – with a blade. They are relentless killers, born of the wild hunt, and are often gifted dark trappings to assist in their missions – hell-forged swords, demonic steeds, packs of hounds, and phantom coaches amongst them. The fires of hell itself burn bright around the huntsmen when their quarry is near, although it is said to be an ill omen indeed even to look upon such a spirit when he is about his grim business, whether or not you are the target.

Irving remembered Baltus Van Tassel's book of spells – had the old man even realized what he had? He shuddered – so far from home, in the place that birthed the evil Hessian, he wished he had brought that book with him, rather than entrust it to the club. However, his own notes and sketches proved invaluable to the Grimms, and soon they began to formulate plans of their own – plans to replicate Irving's victory over the Hessian in their own land.

The Brothers Grimm and their Books of Lore

Though younger than Irving by a few years, Jacob and Wilhelm Grimm were nonetheless possessed of brilliant minds, and an unquenchable thirst for knowledge. They had the uncanny knack of looking beyond the mundane and seeing the wondrous, even the supernatural, and had taken inspiration for their stories to date not only from folklore but also from their own experience. They thrilled Irving with their tales of hunting giants through the wilderness, bringing to justice an evil, cannibalistic witch, and slaying a dread werewolf who preyed on local children. They showed Irving evidence of their claims, and more besides, for they followed in a tradition set down by the French folklorist Charles Perrault, who also recorded his ghost-hunting exploits as cautionary tales, to be passed down to the children of future generations, so as to make them eternally wary of the monsters that exist beyond the veil of our mortal existence.

The Perrault Manuscripts, documenting dozens of monsters and evil spirits supposedly destroyed by Charles Perrault a century earlier, were just the start of the bizarre things the Grimms revealed. Their great contemporary, Hans Christian Anderson, was a part of the same tradition, and indeed the three of them had collaborated on a hunt in Denmark just two years prior, where they had brought down a stone-skinned troll that was stealing goats from the local farmers' herds. The production of the troll's granite fangs was enough to convince Irving that his hosts spoke the truth.

The Grimms brought forth further manuscripts – magical texts from Dee, Copernicus, and Agrippa amongst them, and a whole world of esoteric lore began to unfold before Irving's eyes. Jacob and Wilhelm impressed upon Irving that his contribution to their knowledge was great indeed, and that he could help them further. They invited him to stay with them until May Eve – *Walpurgisnacht,* "the Night of the Burning Witches." On such a night, the spirits walked abroad, and the Grimms were determined to return to Dresden and, along with Washington Irving, hunt the Grey Horseman.

The Wild Hunt

The search began in the old town of Königsbrück, to the north of Dresden. There, in a small churchyard, the Grimms believed they had found the grave of the man dubbed Hans Jagendteufel, who had supposedly murdered his entire family and then, years later, committed suicide. He had been acquitted of all charges during his lifetime, but the guilt had toppled him over the edge – however, he had avoided the guillotine only to be curse to an eternity as the Grey Huntsman. The Grimms had collected stories of the huntsman's appearance stretching back to 1600, and although he usually hunted the guilty, many innocent bystanders had been harmed or even killed just by virtue of seeing the ghostly figure – such is the capricious whim of the dark forces that control the headless revenants.

Irving, naturally, asked who was controlling the huntsman – was it some mortal, as had been the case in Sleepy Hollow? The Grimms looked at each other, and Jacob answered "No. While the head remains lost, only the devil can control the Horseman."

Thus, that night, the three young men set about digging up the remains of the man who had become Hans Jagendteufel. They were quick and discreet about their work, for desecrating holy ground in such a way was a serious crime, and they would doubtless have been accused of bodysnatching if caught. However, the three conspirators believed that the Grey Huntsman had been unable to find his head due to its being buried in consecrated ground, which headless revenants are unable to cross.

Before long, the body was exhumed. Sure enough, the neck of the skeleton was snapped – probably from a noose rather than in any attempt at decapitation. Irving argued that this would not be sufficient to transform the man into a revenant, but the Grimms countered, saying that the folklore was clear – it was the deeds of the man in life that created a headless horseman, not decapitation. After all, had not the Hessian been a monster long before he had lost his head? Satisfied, Irving helped the Brothers Grimm remove the

skull and rebury the body before the first strains of dawn's light streamed over the village.

They stayed two more nights in Königsbrück, taking them up to May 31 – Walpurgisnacht. A few of the locals made great bonfires, and children ran about the streets after dark much as they did in New York upon the night of Halloween, but for the three hunters this was no time for games. Taking up weapons and supplies, and carefully packing the skull, they set off into the forest, on the precarious trail to the clearing known as Lost Waters. The hike took hours, and was arduous indeed in the dark. However, they reached the clearing by midnight as planned, and split up so that they each might cover a different quadrant of the area. According to local legend, the Grey Horseman passed through this way, crossing the ford on his way to claim the soul of a murderer, and so here the three scholars waited for their moment.

Sure enough, not long after midnight, a strange sense of dread pervaded the little clearing. Mist rose from the ground and the temperature fell as sharply as if it were the depths of winter. Frost formed on the coarse undergrowth, and the sound of a hunting horn blasted from somewhere deep in the forest. Irving kept his eyes upon the clearing, trying hard not to succumb to his nerves, and, as expected, soon was heard the sound of hoof beats, drawing ever closer.

The Grey Huntsman plunged from the dark shadow of the forest, drawing to a halt, his pale horse stamping angrily upon the frost-hardened ground. The headless rider wore a long grey coat of noble styling, and had a horn slung across his back. By the huntsman's side was a long saber, for which his hand now reached as though the revenant sensed the ambush.

At a barked signal from Johan, the three ghost hunters emerged from their hiding place. Johan held aloft the skull, and recited words from an Enochian ritual. Wilhelm advanced upon the huntsman, pitchfork in hand in case of attack, while Washington busied himself with bible and holy water, consecrating the ground so that the revenant might be laid to rest at last. At this, the huntsman put up a determined fight. The horse charged at Johan, striking him with its hooves and causing him to drop the skull. To their dismay and surprise, the horse then stamped upon the skull, crushing it to powder – something was terribly wrong.

Before Johan could be injured, Wilhelm leapt forward, stabbing the huntsman through the side with the pitchfork, and dragging him from the horse. Quick as a flash, the huntsman fought to his feet, sword in hand, and made to strike Wilhelm's head from his body. But Irving acted just as quickly. In a trice, he rushed at the huntsman and, using his gold watch-chain that he had worn as surety against the Dullahan, looped it around the huntsman's sword-arm at the wrist, and pulled. The gold cut through the revenant's wrist like a cheese-wire, and the twitching hand fell at once to the ground, sword and all. At this, the huntsman flailed backwards and knocked Irving to the

(OPPOSITE)
Wilhelm and Jacob Grimm were not just writers of fables, but hunters of supernatural entities too! Their battles against the occult were chronicled in the *Books of Grimm*, copies of which are held in chapters of the Lycean Club across the globe.

ground, before mounting his horse once more with incredible agility. He took up his hunting horn with his good hand, and blared upon it three times, causing fire to blaze from its end, before the huntsman, horse and all, vanished – turned to nought but mist on the night air. The three hunters were shaken but unharmed. They found the huntsman's sword lying in the grass, ice-cold to the touch. Of the revenant's hand, there was no sign.

Irving and the Grimms returned to Königsbrück to consult the rest of their books. They knew that they had made a fatal error – the body that they had thought belonged to the huntsman was not the right one, and thus the head had not been what the huntsman sought. As long as it remained lost, the Grey Huntsman would ride again. The possibility that someone might already possess the head, and be controlling the revenant, was too terrible to think about. On this occasion, at least, the Brothers Grimm had to accept defeat – although they kept the sword, which they felt might yet have secrets to give up.

A week later, Irving bade farewell to the Brothers Grimm, and set off for Paris, and thence back to Birmingham. He had been inducted into an elite group of folklorists, who knew of the hidden threats behind the veil of normality, and tried in subtle ways to teach everyday folk about them. Irving knew that he had to make his tale, *The Legend of Sleepy Hollow*, famous – he was now part of a tradition stretching back over a hundred years, and his story would serve to warn others of the dangers present in the dark places in the world.

Chapter 4 - To the Ends of the Earth

After *The Legend of Sleepy Hollow* was published to great acclaim, and Irving had returned at last to America to present his findings to the New York Lycean, he was given sufficient resources to continue his research into headless revenants. He remained in close contact with the Brothers Grimm, exchanging letters and theories for many years, and together they uncovered evidence suggesting that this strange form of decapitated entity had been found the world over, in myriad forms throughout history, from ancient Rome to present-day Brazil. What interested Irving the most was the idea that he could find the source of the haunting – the legend that would provide the origin of the revenants, and perhaps give a clue as to how to dispatch them for good. This was easier said than done, however, as Irving found many legends of distinctive prominence that were all likely contenders.

Irving found that the Far East was particularly rife with ghost stories and superstition, of a kind often unfathomable to westerners. However, the headless revenants had made their presence known there too. In a battered and roughly translated copy of the Chinese *Shan-hai Ching*, for example, Irving found a lengthy discussion of a deity named Xing Tian. Originally written around the fourth century, the myth recalls a much earlier time, during which the giant Xing Tian conducted a battle against "the Supreme Divinity" (which Irving supposed was the Chinese interpretation of his own Christian God). In the battle, Xing Tian was beheaded and his head was buried within Changyang Mountain, but this did not stop him. Xing Tian rose again, this time sprouting eyes in place of his nipples and a mouth in place of a navel. He carried a sharp axe in one hand and a shield in the other, and continued the fight for all eternity, while searching for his missing head.

Although the strange transformation of Xing Tian's body was new to Irving, the account was ancient, and the scholar wondered if perhaps this was the first instance of a headless revenant in the world. Could it really have been inadvertently created by God? And if so, could there be parallels with the Biblical tale of the Fall of Lucifer? Irving shuddered at this, for his research was leading him to wonder if he truly had battled the devil that fateful night in Sleepy Hollow.

Stranger still but no less disturbing, Irving discovered, were the *Nukekubi* of Japan, also called "The Prowling Heads." By day, a Nukekubi is largely indistinguishable from an ordinary person, save for several lines of small wrinkles at the bottom of its neck, almost impossible for the untrained eye to recognize. At night, however, its head detaches from the neck and flies away, preying on mortal flesh. Once it has found its victim, the head emits a paralyzing scream before closing for the kill. Often the Nukekubi have no idea what they are; they might only recall dreams in which they fly around rooms or hear frightened screams. To vanquish a Nukekubi, its idle body must be hunted at night and destroyed, thereby also killing the head. This is one of the more horrific headless revenant legends, for the Nukekubi appear to be alive, and largely innocent – their curse cannot be broken except by their own death. Whatever these creatures were, Irving decided, they were not what he sought – they had little in common with the horsemen he had encountered.

Another supposed "living" headless creature was detailed by the ancient Greek philosopher Pliny, and then documented centuries later. These were the Blemmyae – supposedly an African tribe, with no heads, but with faces on their chests. They were also veritable giants, standing "eight feet tall and eight feet wide," meaning that their characteristics had much in common with Xing Tian, who was written about only 200 years later. Sketches of the Blemmyae, amongst other creatures, accompanied copies of a 14th-century manuscript entitled *The Travels of Sir John Mandeville.* These records, written first-hand by an English knight, first circulated in 1356, and in them Mandeville claims to have met the Blemmyae, writing:

> *There are many different kinds of people in these idles. In one, there is a race of great stature, like giants, foul and horrible to look at; they have one eye only, in the middle of their foreheads. They eat raw flesh and raw fish. In another part, there are ugly folk without heads, who have eyes in each shoulder; their mouths are round, like a horseshoe, in the middle of their chest. In yet another part there are headless men whose eyes and mouths are on their backs.*

This third race recorded by Mandeville was also mentioned by Pliny. The veracity of the claims was in much doubt, of course, and even in the 19th century Irving could find no verification. But he had to wonder if Mandeville had really seen those headless giants, and if so, into what circle of hell he had strayed while on his long voyage.

Returning again to a possible divine origin for these headless monsters, Irving stumbled across a reference to a headless deity in the Hindu religion of India. After much research, he pieced together several translations of sacred texts that made mention of the Hindu goddess *Chinnamasta,* or "She Whose Head is Severed." She is depicted carrying her own severed head on a platter, its mouth open as it swallows the blood which sprays from the stump of her

(Opposite)
Xing Tian, a ferocious headless giant from China, has eyes in the place of nipples and a mouth instead of a navel.

(Opposite)
By day, the *Nukekubi* look like normal people, but by night the heads detach, screaming through the night until they find human prey to attack.

neck. Her devotees are usually nearby, also catching the goddess's blood in their mouths. The legend goes that Chinnamasta decapitated herself so that she could feed her hungry servants with her own blood. She stands demonstrating that life and death are inextricably linked.

Again, Irving tried to make some correlation between this tale and the others – was this divine blood responsible for the spread of headless revenants since ancient times, like some infectious disease? The vampiric nature of the Japanese Prowling Heads might suggest a link – but how could this information help him in his ongoing investigation? Irving researched Hindu ritual and symbols thoroughly as he strove to make his esoteric defenses against the predations of headless spirits as ironclad as possible. He might not understand the root of the mystery, he decided, but he could be prepared for any eventuality.

It was some relief when his studies returned to the history of the Americas, even if the subject of those studies was of the disturbing kind. Irving received a note from a novitiate within the Lycean who had traveled to South America to investigate reports of Catholic miracles in a small church in Brazil. While there, the student had heard a strange tale of a headless spirit, which he thought would interest Irving. He had dutifully conducted interviews and gathered what evidence he could from the simple people of the local parish. They called this entity the *Mula Sem Cabeça,* or "headless mule": a monstrous mule with a hellish flame where its head should be. Its horseshoes were made of silver and made a terrifying sound as it galloped. Even though it had no head, the mule could be heard neighing from a great distance away, and sometimes these sounds transformed into human-like screams and wails.

The God-fearing villagers swore to the Lycean novitiate that the mules were created when a woman had a romantic relationship with a priest – she was transformed due to her sinful seduction of a man of the cloth. However, other parishioners believed that sex before marriage, sacrilege, or even infanticide could also lead to a woman being cursed to become the mule. Digging deep into the church records, the student found an older version of the tale, written by a monk in the late 17th century. In this version of events, the headless mule was a noblewoman who often visited the local cemetery in the middle of the night. One night, her husband followed her and was horrified to discover his wife feasting upon a corpse. As the villagers learned of the woman's dark secret and rounded on her, she was cursed, transforming into a monster and galloping into the woods, never to return.

It was said that the Mula Sem Cabeça would appear if someone ran in front of a cross at midnight. Anything that crossed the path of the monster – man or beast – was trampled and killed, or maimed by having its eyes sucked out by magical means. The only way to hide from the mule was to throw oneself face down on the ground, hiding nails, teeth, and anything that might gleam in the dark.

Chinnamasta does not have many worshipers due to her intense nature, though the faithful maintain that shocking imagery is the best way to break through mental barriers to the truth.

The story amused Irving, and with no solid evidence he could not be sure if there was any truth to it. But he felt most uncomfortable at the similarities between tales of the Mula Sem Cabeça and other headless revenants from isolated legends around the world – the headless horse (or mule, in this case), the God-given curse, the hellfire … Irving crossed himself against the evil spirits that he felt compelled to study.

American Gothic

With no clear candidate for the origins of the headless revenants, Irving instead set out to combat the entities on a case-by-case basis, using the knowledge he had gathered over the preceding years. It was in his homeland that he encountered some of the more persistent spirits, for North America had long been a homeland of far-flung immigrants, all bringing with them diverse beliefs and religious practices. Irving set out to learn as much as he could about America's own headless spirits.

In his later years, Irving recorded some 15 headless ghosts in the New York area alone, three of them akin to the Headless Horseman of Sleepy Hollow.

In North Carolina, Irving went in search of Blackbeard's ghost, reputedly to be found in Teach's Hole, Ocracoke Island. It was there that Blackbeard – the pirate Edward Teach – made his famous last stand against the Royal Navy. Such was Blackbeard's notoriety that the naval commander, Lieutenant Maynard, ordered Teach's head struck off to ensure that he was dead. As the body hit the water, the head supposedly cried: "Come on Edward," and the headless body swam three times around the ship before sinking to the bottom.

From that day to this, Blackbeard's ghost has haunted Teach's Hole, forever searching for his missing head. Sometimes, the headless ghost floats on the surface of the water, or swims around Teach's Hole, glowing under the water. Sometimes, people see a strange light coming from the shore, which locals dub "Teach's light."

A device of grim execution, the guillotine is responsible for many headless ghosts – from the nobles of revolutionary France to the sinister slave-spirits of Wytheville, Virginia.

When he had visited Paris, France, Irving had found more civilized tales of headless spirits – those of Marie Antoinette and King Louis XVI foremost amongst them. These had appeared to be little more than regular ghosts – restless spirits of those who had died before their time, with no real power over the living other than occasionally to manifest, heads tucked under their arms. The guillotine had claimed many heads in France at the end of the previous century, and so it was to be expected that ghosts would walk the sites of their execution or interment still. However, Irving was surprised to find a ghostly tale of the guillotine in his own land, presenting him with one of the more intriguing American ghost stories.

In 1850, aged 67, Irving visited Wytheville, Virginia, where the owner of a manor house reported being haunted by a plethora of headless ghosts, who were making his life a misery. Irving discovered that the manor stood on the site of an old cabin built by a man called Joseph Baker. Mr. Baker had supposedly promised two of his slaves their freedom upon his death, but the two slaves decided to hurry this along and not only murdered their owner, but added him to a corn mash they were making. When news of the crime got out, the two slaves were captured and killed on the property.

While investigating the manor, Irving discovered a hidden cellar, undoubtedly from the foundations of the old cabin that had not been filled in. Within this damp, fetid room they found a working guillotine, rusted with age and still bearing a crust of dried blood. Buried beneath the floor were half a dozen skulls – it would seem that someone had found a barbaric method of executing unwanted slaves in the early days of the house. Irving declared that the headless ghosts were not demonic entities, but restless spirits – when the gruesome guillotine was dismantled and the cellar consecrated, the hauntings quietened, though they never fully stopped.

El Muerto – Irving's Final Case

In 1859, at the end of Irving's career as a psychical detective and just months before his death, he was summoned once more from his idyllic home at Sunnyside, Sleepy Hollow, this time to Texas. There, soldiers garrisoning Fort Inge on the San Antonio–El Paso road had reported sighting a headless man on a grey horse, riding hell-for-leather along the trail. The phantom rider had supposedly appeared outside the nearby townsteads several times before, and each time had presaged a violent shooting or outbreak of fever in the settlements. No longer a young man, Irving nevertheless felt compelled to investigate and so, taking up his books and ghost-hunting paraphernalia one last time, he set off westward.

Once in San Antonio, Irving quickly learned the tale of a Mexican bandit by the name of Vidal, who had plied his trade in a part of South Texas known as "No Man's Land" some ten years earlier. His illicit business led him on a collision course with the fledgling Texas Rangers, which did not end well for Vidal.

(OPPOSITE)
The *Mula sem Cabeça* of Brazil is a ghostly, black mule with silver horseshoes. It has a bridle attached to thin air where its head should be, and breathes fire from its neck!

Two Texas Rangers, Taylor Creed and William "Big Foot" Wallace, were bandit-hunters without peer, who often resorted to brutal means to dissuade the bandits from returning to their territory. When Vidal stole a herd of cattle and two prize mustangs that belonged to Creed, he earned himself a particularly sticky end. When the posse caught up with the outlaws, they attacked at nightfall, killing Vidal and the bandits in their sleep. But this was not enough – Taylor and Wallace wanted to make an example of the audacious Vidal. Big Foot beheaded Vidal and lashed his body to a saddle on the back of a horse. He attached Vidal's severed head to the saddle, still wearing its sombrero, and turned the mustang loose.

The pirate Edward Teach, more famously called Blackbeard, still searches for his missing head around Teach's Hole in North Carolina.

Soon stories started to circulate about a headless rider roaming the hill country. It was seen by numerous cowboys, Indians, and soldiers, and before long each new sighting reported that the Horseman was riddled with bullet-holes and arrows. Local homesteaders began to call this headless horseman "*El*

Muerto." As time went by a legend grew that people must avoid this strange apparition, for if it was seen some evil misfortune would befall them.

It was a familiar tale to Irving, but at first he doubted he could do anything – after all, if the body and head of the Horseman were still animated, then there were no remains for him to use in a ritual, and no head with which to compel El Muerto to leave the earthly realm. However, soon he learned more to the story. A local preacher told Irving that a group of ranchers had caught up with the poor burdened horse near Alice, Texas – it had indeed been shot with gun and arrow, but the horse was quite alive. They had buried Vidal's body in an unmarked grave near the tiny community of Ben Bolt. However, that was not the end of the sightings. As soon as the body was laid to rest, soldiers at Fort Inge began to see an apparition of the headless rider, and mysterious deaths within the communities around No Man's Land quickly followed each new sighting. It seemed that El Muerto was a headless revenant after all!

Knowing that the local lay preacher would not be enough for the battle to come, Irving sent word to the south for a Catholic missionary named Father Bermudez. When Bermudez arrived in No Man's Land, the two men set about planning their attack. First, they traveled to Ben Bolt and spoke to one of the ranchers who had found Vidal's horse years earlier. He was a tired old man, the last of the three ranchers, the others all having succumbed to El Muerto's curse. Nonetheless, the hardy old cowboy led Irving and Bermudez to the spot where he'd buried Vidal's body. Next to the grave, a large, gnarled tree had sprung up impossibly quickly, casting a grim shadow over the place. Before night fell, Irving and Bermudez instructed some local ranch-hands to dig up the body – all were shocked to discover that it had not fully decomposed, and still had seemingly living flesh sloughing from its bones. Irving dug deep into his reserve of fortitude and took up the rotting head, wrapping it in sackcloth before closing up the coffin.

That night, the two hunters waited by the crossroads in No Man's Land, a stone's throw from Fort Inge, where El Muerto was most often seen. Sure enough, just as in the forests of Germany, the sound of hoof beats was heard shortly after midnight, echoing across the plain. This time, Irving was in no doubt that he had the correct skull in his possession, although he still shook with fear at the recollection at how close he had come to death upon his last meeting with such a revenant.

This time, when El Muerto appeared, thundering from the dusty plain with fire dancing around the hooves of his mustang, it was Irving who stepped before the phantom. Holding aloft the head and reciting ritual words from the writings of Dr John Dee, he faced down the revenant, who brought his horse about, stomping and braying in frustration. From behind El Muerto stepped Father Bermudez, holding aloft a golden crucifix and reciting the cant of exorcism against the devil's servant.

(OPPOSITE)
Said to be the ghost of Vidal, a cattle rustler who was decapitated by Texas Rangers, *El Muerto*, the "Headless One," now rides a grey mustang across the plains, his body riddled with bullet-holes and Indian arrows.

At this two-pronged attack, the power of El Muerto visibly lessened, his stature shrinking away. The horse bucked and threw the headless rider, before galloping away, vanishing into a cloud of dust. The revenant flailed, firing spectral pistols at the two ghost hunters, but the ethereal bullets had no effect. Slowly but surely, El Muerto was pacified, until he stood silent and placid before Washington Irving.

Irving completed the ritual, buoyed by his efforts so far and growing in courage. He handed the skull to the headless rider, with one last command – that El Muerto should leave the earthly plain and find peace in the afterlife. At these words, the form of El Muerto, head and all, fell away into dust and shadow, until Irving and Bermudez were alone on the plain.

Irving's Legacy

The victory over El Muerto was to be Irving's last in the field. Every physical encounter with the headless revenants increased his knowledge, but took a heavy toll on him, and he knew that one man could not go on forever fighting evil in such a fashion. Whatever vigor flowed in the veins of the Grimms was not endowed on him – he was but a man. Instead, he turned his attention to recording his endeavors for future generations. He wrote stories, as he had promised the Grimms he would, but he also sent an unprecedented body of research to the Lycean Club, so that future generations of psychical detectives and ghost hunters could draw upon his research in times of need. Thus did Washington Irving's legacy of battling evil forces endure forever.

Here lies the gentle humorist, who died
In the bright Indian Summer of his fame!
A simple stone, with but a date and name,
Marks his secluded resting-place beside
The river that he loved and glorified.
Here in the autumn of his days he came,
But the dry leaves of life were all aflame
With tints that brightened and were multiplied.
How sweet a life was his; how sweet a death!
Living, to wing with mirth the weary hours,
Or with romantic tales the heart to cheer;
Dying, to leave a memory like the breath
Of summers full of sunshine and of showers,
A grief and gladness in the atmosphere.

– Henry Wadsworth Longfellow, on Washington Irving
In the Churchyard at Tarrytown, 187

Legacy of the Horseman

Though none can say for sure just how effective Washington Irving's cautionary tale proved, it cannot be disputed that the popularity of the tale has created an enduring appetite for stories of Sleepy Hollow and Headless Horsemen. Several adaptations of Irving's story have been created for the screen, most notably perhaps the Tim Burton Gothic horror movie *Sleepy Hollow* (1999), which portrayed Johnny Depp's Ichabod Crane as an anachronistic forensics expert trying to uncover a conspiracy in the old Dutch colony. In more recent years, the story has inspired a television series of the same name, which pits a resurrected and temporally displaced Ichabod against a host of supernatural mysteries in modern-day America.

The tale – and its source material of decapitated ghost stories from around the world – has inspired not only books, films, and even musicals, but also urban legends. Today, stories of headless motorcyclists are more common than horsemen, with similar tales from as far afield as the Elmore, Ohio, and Kasara Ghat, India. These apocryphal stories often take the same format – surprising given heir geographical spread. A lone motorcyclist (sometimes part of a biker gang) is killed while overtaking a truck on a tight, remote road. He's forced from the road by oncoming traffic, and is beheaded in the resulting crash. The site of the accident is always a notorious black spot, and from that day forward the biker rides up and down the road as a dire warning to others, or perhaps seeking vengeance on lazy road planners. A headless biker in Tulare, California, supposedly boasts not only firsthand eyewitnesses, but also living relatives of the unfortunate victim who testify to the phenomenon.

This urban legend has itself been adapted several times into other media. For example, a headless rider was featured in the cartoon series *The Real Ghostbusters*, while the cult TV show, *Kolchak: the Night Stalker*, featured a headless biker seeking revenge against the rival gang that murdered him. More famously, however, Marvel Comics created the character Ghost Rider – first as a spectral cowboy in the Wild West, and then more popularly as the leather-clad, skull-faced vigilante who hunts down evil souls and sends them to the underworld. Though not technically headless, when the Rider's host transforms, his head becomes a grinning skull wreathed in flame, and his motorcycle an infernal engine carried on wheels of fire. Other comic-book creations, such as the Spider-man nemesis Jack O'Lantern, and the Green Goblin with his pumpkin bombs, undoubtedly owe much to the Legend of Sleepy Hollow.

(OVERLEAF)
A latter-day spirit of vengeance? A restless spirit left earthbound by a tragic motor accident? Or a fiction created by modern-day readers of Irving's stories? In any case, the ominous sound of approaching hooves seems to have been replaced by the gunning of phantasmal engines; the legend of the Headless Rider lives on!

We now live in a world where the essence of the tale – the 'high concept' – has saturated much of our popular entertainment, from children's books to movies, comics to rock songs. Sleepy Hollow is not just a modern legend from the United States, but an iconic ghost story known around the world. While few believe that the tale is anything other than fiction, perhaps Washington Irving was not wholly unsuccessful in his mission. For who today, when faced with approaching hoofbeats in a misty forest at night, would do anything other than hide from the dread rider that approaches? And of course, what now exists of the Apollonian Club, and its sister Lycean? Perhaps there are guardians still, watching and waiting for the appearance of dread spirits with which to do battle...

Glossary

APPARITION A ghostlike image of a person.
COINCIDENCE A concurrence of events without apparent causal connection.
CONSECRATE To make something sacred.
DEMONIC Characteristic of demons or evil spirits.
ENTITY Something that has a distinct existence.
ESOTERIC Something that is understood by only a small number of people with a specialized knowledge or interest.
FOREBODING A premonition of something bad.
FORMIDABLE Inspiring fear or respect by being powerful.
LUMINESCENCE The emission of light by a substance.
MANIFEST To display or demonstrate by an act or appearance.
MELANCHOLY A feeling of sadness, usually with no obvious cause.
NEFARIOUS A wicked or criminal action.
OCCULT Supernatural, mystical, or magical beliefs, practices, or phenomena.
PAGAN A person who has religious beliefs other than those of the main world.
PEDAGOGUE A strict or pedantic teacher.
PHENOMENON A fact or situation that exists or has happened.
PILLAGE To rob a place using violence, especially in wartime.
POSSESSED Controlled by an evil spirit.
PRETERNATURAL Beyond what is normal or natural.
REVENANT A person who has returned from the dead.
SPECTRAL Ghostlike.
THEORIZE To create a theoretical premise or framework for something.

For More Information

American Society for Psychical Research, Inc. (ASPR)
5 West 73rd Street
New York, NY 10023
(212) 799-5050
Web site: http://www.aspr.com
This organization's mission is to explore extraordinary or unexplained phenomena that have been called psychic or paranormal, and their implications for our understanding of consciousness, the universe, and the nature of existence. It addresses questions with scientific research and offers educational activities including lectures and conferences.

Ghost Hunters
Syfy Channel
NBCUniversal Cable Entertainment Group
30 Rockefeller Plaza
New York, NY - 10112
(212) 664-4444
http://www.syfy.com/ghosthunters
In each episode of the Ghost Hunters television program, Jason Hawes and his team of paranormal investigators, TAPS (The Atlantic Paranormal Society) investigate paranormal activity across the country.

Parapsychological Association, Inc. (PA)
P.O. Box 24173
Columbus, OH 43224
(202) 318-2364
Web site: http://www.parapsych.org
The Parapsychological Association is the international professional organization of scientists and scholars

engaged in the study of "psi" (or "psychic") experiences, such as telepathy, clairvoyance, and psychic healing. The PA endorses no ideologies or beliefs other than the value of rigorous scientific and scholarly inquiry.

WEBSITES

Because of the changing nature of internet links, Rosen Publishing has developed an online list of websites related to the subject of this book. This site is updated regularly. Please use this link to access the list:

http://www.rosenlinks.com/MH/headless

For Further Reading

Brown, Nathan R. *The Mythology of Grimm: The Fairy Tale and Folklore Roots of the Popular TV Show.* New York, NY: Berkley Boulevard Books, 2014.

Buckland, Raymond. *The Weiser Field Guide to Ghosts: Apparitions, Spirits, Spectral Lights, and Other Hauntings of History and Legend.* San Francisco, CA: Weiser Books, 2009.

Burstein, Andrew. *The Original Knickerbocker: The Life of Washington Irving.* New York: NY: Basic Books, 2008.

Irvine, Alexander, and Washington Irving. *The Secret Journal of Ichabod Crane.* New York, NY: Three Rivers Press, 2014.

Irving, Washington, and Charles Neider. *The Complete Tales of Washington Irving.* New York, NY: Da Capo Press, 1998.

Irving, Washington. *History, Tales, and Sketches.* New York, NY: The Viking Press, 1983.

Irving, Washington. *The Legend of Sleepy Hollow and Other Stories.* Mineola, NY: Dover Publications, 2008.

Jones, Brian J. *Washington Irving: The Definitive Biography of America's First Bestselling Author.* New York, NY: Arcade Publishing, 2011.

Matthews, Rupert. *The Little Book of the Paranormal.* Stroud, Glouchestershire, England: History Press, 2010.

Straub, Peter. *Ghost Story.* New York, NY: Berkley Books, 2016.

Wayland, M. J. *50 Real American Ghost Stories: A Journey Into the Haunted History of the United States: 1800-1899.* Salt Spring Island, Canada: 2013.

Index